GEORGE WHITFIELD

An Introduction to
DRAMA

SECOND EDITION

OXFORD UNIVERSITY PRESS

Oxford University Press, Ely House, London W. 1

GLASGOW   NEW YORK   TORONTO   MELBOURNE   WELLINGTON
CAPE TOWN   SALISBURY   IBADAN   NAIROBI   LUSAKA   ADDIS ABABA
BOMBAY   CALCUTTA   MADRAS   KARACHI   LAHORE   DACCA
KUALA LUMPUR   HONG KONG

FIRST EDITION 1938
REPRINTED FIVE TIMES
SECOND EDITION 1963
REPRINTED 1964, 1965, 1966

PRINTED IN GREAT BRITAIN

PREFACE

THE year 430 B.C. was the probable date of the first play in this book and the last appeared in A.D. 1955. In one volume plays are included which gain much from comparison although they are set so widely apart in chronology that they are usually found only in several. As the aim of the book is to become an instrument of teaching rather than a definitive statement, it has been possible to cover this wide range without making the treatment superficial. Topics which call for a fuller examination than is possible in a volume of this size have been put as questions among the *Points for Discussion* at the end of the extracts, where they may form the beginning of a comprehensive survey by teacher and students. The rest of these questions lead towards a fuller appreciation of the dramatic significance of the passages to which they refer. No attempt is made in the brief introductions to the chapters to give an exhaustive study of the plays which follow; the aim is rather to draw attention to the conditions which made such plays possible.

A beginning is made with Classical drama. It has exercised an immense influence on English plays without, for the most part, determining their form; and it is possible to understand English plays much more fully when they are studied together with others which were at once so great and so different.

In making the selection from English drama, emphasis has been placed throughout on plays which have marked some new development in the relations of audience, theatre, and dramatist. This explains the notable omission of Sheridan and Goldsmith in favour of George Lillo and the authors of melodrama. *The School for Scandal* and *She Stoops to Conquer*, though they were comedies of manners which have achieved lasting fame, did not represent something new in the theatre like *George Barnwell* and *The Murder in the Red Barn*. Because he can fairly be regarded as the founder of modern drama, Ibsen is included; and the best examples of Expressionism on the English stage are the plays of the Brothers Čapek in translation.

Drama is a social art. No one can produce a play by himself. The words of the text are not the play, nor is the theatre in which it will eventually be produced. Even a dress rehearsal can hardly be called a performance. A play is the cumulative product of many relationships, and it is these relationships which have been made the basis of the study of drama in this survey.

G. J. N. W.

The author gratefully acknowledges permission to reprint the following copyright passages: to the Cambridge University Press, for Sophocles, *Oedipus Tyrannus*, translated by Mr. J. T. Sheppard; Messrs. Gerald Howe, Ltd., for *Maria Marten*, edited by Mr. Montagu Slater; the Oxford University Press, for *An Enemy of the People* by Ibsen, translated by James Walter McFarlane, and for *The Insect Play*, by the Brothers Čapek; the late Mr. Bernard Shaw, for *Saint Joan*; Messrs. Faber & Faber, Ltd., for *Murder in the Cathedral* by T. S. Eliot and *Waiting for Godot* by Samuel Beckett.

CONTENTS

LIST OF PLATES

INTRODUCTION

IT is a day of great importance in the life of a child when he first realizes that one and one make two. The intuition with which he seizes the relationship between one and two becomes the first link in a whole chain of scientific reasoning. It is a day of equal importance when he first appreciates the significance of the words 'Once upon a time . . .' or 'Let's pretend . . .', and knows that something will follow which will prove uniquely satisfying. The wildest improbabilities are accepted without demur: bears speak, pigs build houses, and giants roam the country-side; but in the midst of all these improbabilities, certain things must remain constant: there are three bears, and the youngest has the most surprising news to report; there are three pigs, and it is the third who defeats the wolf; and if the giant should encounter the hero, then his great strength is never of final avail.

As the child grows older, the fact that one and one make two remains constant; they can never in any circumstances make two and a half. The significance of the words 'Once upon a time . . .' or 'Let's pretend . . .' does not remain constant. The words themselves are still there, even if they are not always said aloud, for every time a man picks up a novel he is saying to himself 'Once upon a time . . .', and every time he goes to the theatre he is saying 'Let's pretend . . .'. But he does not expect that his novel will have a simple plot in which the youngest son is always more successful than his elder brothers, and in the theatre his imagination will no longer transform a saucepan into a helmet, or a dilapidated curtain into a sultan's robe. He goes to the theatre prepared to make some allowances: he knows that although the play may be about the reign of Elizabeth, the people all around him will be wearing clothes which very obviously have come from twentieth-century shops, and that only on the stage will the theatre at all resemble the age of Shakespeare. He accepts this, in the same way as the child accepts the assumption that the bears can talk; but, like the child, he also has his demands. Although the orchestra in front of them may be wearing boiled shirts, the actors themselves must be dressed in full Elizabethan costume, and must talk only of the things which were known to that age; an allusion to wireless would ruin the play, although an amplifier may be hanging overhead.

The study of what people are prepared to accept when they go to the theatre is full of interest, because they are not always prepared to accept the same kind of things. The Elizabethans were quite content to see Julius Caesar come on to the stage in doublet and hose, dressed like one of themselves. A few years ago the experiment was made of acting some of Shakespeare's plays in modern dress, and King Claudius offered Hamlet a whisky and soda instead of a goblet of wine. The experiment aroused interest by its novelty, but it was not a success; the audiences were not prepared to 'pretend' in that kind of way. This is an obvious change, and other differences are more subtle, existing side by side in the same age. Operas and musical plays demand that we shall assume for the moment that people express themselves in songs and in choruses as well as in ordinary speech. Having made this assumption, in itself so extraordinary, an audience is less likely to quibble over other surprising happenings, and it is a fact that in most musical plays the plot abounds in incidents far removed from the probabilities of real life. Nevertheless, once the dramatist has shown the audience the way in which he wants them to 'pretend', they expect him to continue in this way. They are quite willing to enjoy a farce, packed full of absurdities, with the characters behaving as if they had stepped out of *Alice in Wonderland*; but they do not expect these figures of fun to behave in the second half of the play like ordinary men and women any more than, when they look at their newspaper, they expect to see a photograph placed among the caricatures of a cartoon.

The things in a theatre or in a play which people are willing to accept as part of the 'Let's pretend . . .', and which they will come to expect as part of the performance, are called the *conventions* of drama. It is a pity that this word 'conventions' has come to mean only good manners in social behaviour, for when it is used of drama the meaning is much bigger. The conventions of drama are not merely rules and methods of the theatre which dramatists have created and followed; they show the angle from which people of different nations and of varying periods have looked out upon life. They point to the popular philosophy and, by showing what it took for granted in interpreting human experience, they form a kind of commentary upon the age which produced them.

Dramatic history is history in one of its most living forms; G. M. Trevelyan has called drama 'the first of arts'. The words of a play are the words to which people have actually listened—these are the characters and these are the thoughts and incidents which a past age considered interesting and significant. It is with this in mind that we can most fully appreciate the words which they have left.

CHAPTER I

PLAYS OF MEN AND FATE

IN Ancient Greece, the conventions of the theatre were rigid; even the plot and the characters were known beforehand by the audience, who watched the play in an attitude of mind quite different from that of a modern theatregoer.

People who attended a theatre in Greece had something in common with a modern audience at the performance of an oratorio like the *Messiah* when it is given in a church. All the people who attend may not be themselves deeply religious, but they know that the theme of the work to which they are listening has a religious significance, and that it is part of a service of worship. The story is well known to them, so they have no concern with the development of an unexpected plot. The principal singers make no attempt to represent the great figures of the Bible by wearing costumes of the period, or even by using language closely imitating that of real life; their aim is to use music and language in a way which will help the audience not to visualize but to imagine the incidents in the work which they are performing. Greek actors had a similar aim, but the place of the music in an oratorio was taken by the rhythmical motion and chanting of the chorus, which will be mentioned again later.

The theatre was theoretically a temple of the god of fertility, Dionysus, with his altar in the centre. It was a huge place in the open air capable of accommodating about 20,000 people, who sat on tiered seats, like the crowd at a football match. The stories of the plays were taken from the religious myths of the heroes and demi-gods who were the founders of the nation, and whose lives had come to have a

ATHENS THE THEATRE OF DIONYSUS FROM THE EAST

significance in Greek religion, even as the lives of the saints and martyrs have come to have a significance in the Christian religion. As the theatre was also a temple, it would have been inappropriate to present murders and deeds of violence on the stage. These were always supposed to happen 'off', and were reported by a narrator, although the screams of the victims might be heard.

With the plot known, the interest which comes from surprise was barred, and other interests were introduced. In the first place, the performances were always made a public holiday, and the huge crowd had a sense of the unity and greatness of their own nation when, as a body, they witnessed the greatest scenes of their history re-enacted before them. With this was the interest which comes from watching a competition, for different playwrights presented plays on the same story, and there was a prize at the end for that adjudged to be the best.

These conditions greatly affected both the manner of performance and the kind of play which was performed. The actors had to be seen by this huge crowd of people, and they moved on a stage which was wide, but shallow. To make them more easily visible, and as a sign that they were more than human, they wore high-soled boots called buskins; and to emphasize their part in the story they wore a mask which represented their typical mood throughout the play. Along with the actors, who were always very few in number, there was a group of people known as the chorus, who acted as a sort of guide to the spectators, commenting on the action, pointing out the significance of what was happening, and sometimes taking part in the play. These actors did not perform on the stage, but on the 'orchestra', a semicircular space in front of the stage, on which was placed the altar to Dionysus. They accompanied their words with a kind of rhythmical walk, and seem to have possessed a unique gift of conveying thought by physical movement.

These were the conditions which determined the kind of plays which the dramatists could write. The knowledge which the audience had of the plot, and the masks worn by the actors, left no scope for development of character. In Shakespeare's play, Macbeth begins as the valorous Thane of Glamis, trusted by his king, and respected by all; he ends as a bloodthirsty tyrant, isolated by his crimes. If he wore the same mask throughout the play, such a development would be impossible. In Greek plays the hero usually acts with the best motives, and in the confident expectation that his actions are virtuous and wise. But, to his horror, he discovers when it is too late that his actions have had an effect utterly different from that which he had expected. There is a contrast between the hero's intentions in his actions and the results which do, in fact, flow from them. The dramatists seized upon this contrast and emphasized it until they were able to arouse in the audience feelings of pity and terror at the spectacle of the gulf which could yawn between a man's intentions and his achievements. The cause of this gulf lay outside him, beyond his control; it was just Nemesis, or Fate, to which even the gods themselves were subject.

Plays like this had a seriousness of purpose which made comic scenes out of place, and there were no sub-plots. The sections of the play were divided by the utterances of the chorus, whose continued presence in front of the stage made it almost impossible for the audience to imagine any considerable change of place for the action, or sudden gap in time. These facts have been called the *Three Unities* of Plot, Place, and Time, but they are not to be taken as rules which the dramatists followed so much as habits which they developed.

One of the most typical stories of Greek tragedy was that of Oedipus, which became an outstanding example of the inscrutable workings of Fate. Even before Oedipus was born, his father, Laius, King of Thebes, learned from an oracle that his son was predestined to kill him. He did all in his power to avoid this doom by exposing his newly born son on the side of Mount Cithaeron with a stake driven through his feet so that he would die. But this very act was used in the fulfilment of the destiny, as Oedipus was rescued by a shepherd of King Polybus of Corinth, and grew up in ignorance of his own father. He was taken to the palace of King Polybus, who brought him up as his own son. In his early manhood, Oedipus began to realize that there was something unusual and irregular in his history, and went to the oracle at Delphi to discover the truth about himself. There he learned that he was destined to kill his father and marry his own mother. Appalled by this revelation, Oedipus did all in his power to avoid committing the crimes which had been prophesied for him; and again the attempts to avoid his destiny were instrumental in its fulfilment. As he thought that Polybus was his father, he resolved never to return to him, and took a road away from Corinth on which he met his own father, Laius, at a cross-roads. They quarrelled, and Laius was slain. In ignorance of the fulfilment of part of the destiny which had been foretold, Oedipus continued his journeys, and was able to deliver the Thebans from the curse of the Sphinx, who put her famous riddle to every Theban who passed by, killing those who could not find the answer: 'What is it that walks on four legs in the morning, on two at noon, and on three in the evening?' The answer, as most people now know, is a man, who begins his life crawling on all fours, walks upright in his maturity, and needs a stick (the third 'leg') in his old age. When Oedipus gave this answer, the

Sphinx destroyed herself. In gratitude for their deliverance, the Thebans made Oedipus king in place of Laius, who had mysteriously disappeared. The last part of his destiny was fulfilled when Oedipus married the queen Jocasta, his mother.

Because of the sins which Oedipus had unknowingly committed, the land was cursed with a terrible plague. As king, he did all in his power to discover the cause of the plague, and when the oracle said that it was the murderer of Laius who was bringing upon Thebes the wrath of the gods, Oedipus called down curses upon the head of the plague-bringer, and redoubled his efforts to discover his identity. Conscious of his own integrity of purpose, Oedipus was utterly blind to the first hints that he was himself implicated in the curse, and it was this situation which was made the core of the drama *Oedipus Tyrannus*, the first of a trilogy of dramas by Sophocles: *Oedipus Tyrannus*, *Oedipus at Colonus*, and the *Antigone*.

At the beginning of the extract, the queen Jocasta is kneeling at the altar of Apollo, beseeching him to show the people of Thebes the cause of the disasters which are befalling them.

THE OEDIPUS TYRANNUS OF SOPHOCLES

Translated by J. T. SHEPPARD

SCENE: *An open place in front of the Royal Palace at Thebes.* JOCASTA *kneels at one of the altars before the Palace in the presence of the* CHORUS *of citizens of Thebes. A* MESSENGER *enters from Corinth.*

MESSENGER. Can you direct me, strangers, to the house
  Of Oedipus, your Master?—Better still,
  Perchance you know where I may find the King?
CHORUS. This is the house, and he within. The Queen,
  His wife and mother of his house, is here.
MESSENGER. His wife, and blest with offspring! Happiness
  Wait on her always, and on all her home!

JOCASTA. I wish you happy too. Your gracious speech
Deserves no less. Tell me with what request
You are come hither, or what news you bring.   10
MESSENGER. Lady, good news for him and all his house.
JOCASTA. Why, what good news is this? Who sent you here?
MESSENGER. I come from Corinth, and have that to tell
I think will please, though it be partly sad.
JOCASTA. How can a sad tale please? Come, tell it me!
MESSENGER. The people of that country, so men said,
Will choose him monarch of Corinthia.
JOCASTA. What? Is old Polybus no longer King?
MESSENGER. No longer King. Death has him in the grave.
JOCASTA. Dead! Say you so? Oedipus' father dead?   20
MESSENGER. If he be not so, may I die myself!
JOCASTA. Quick! To your master, girl; tell him this news!
O oracles of the gods, where are you now?
This was the man that Oedipus so feared
To slay, he needs must leave his country. Dead!
And 'tis not Oedipus, but Fortune slew him!

Enter OEDIPUS

OEDIPUS. Tell me, Jocasta, wife of my dear love,
Why you have called me hither, out of doors.
JOCASTA. Let this man speak; and as you listen, judge
The issue of the god's grand oracles!   30
OEDIPUS. This man, who is he? What has he to tell?
JOCASTA. He comes from Corinth, and will tell you this:—
Polybus is no more. Your father's dead.
OEDIPUS. What! Is this true, sir? Answer for yourself!
MESSENGER. If this must needs come first in my report,
'Tis true enough. King Polybus is dead.
OEDIPUS. By treachery? Or did sickness visit him?
MESSENGER. A little shift of the scale, and old men sleep.
OEDIPUS. Ah! My poor father died, you say, by sickness?
MESSENGER. Yes, and by reason of his length of days.   40
OEDIPUS. Ah me! Wife, why should any man regard

The Delphic Hearth oracular, and the birds
That scream above us—guides, whose evidence
Doomed me to kill my father, who is dead,
Yes, buried under ground, and I stand here,
And have not touched my weapon?—Stay! Perchance
'Twas grief for me. I may have slain him so.
Anyhow, he is dead, and to his grave
Has carried all these oracles—worth nothing!

JOCASTA. Worth nothing. Did I not tell you so long since?   50
OEDIPUS. You told me, but my fears misguided me.
JOCASTA. Banish your fears, and think no more of them.
OEDIPUS. No, no! Should I not fear my mother's bed?
JOCASTA. Why, what should a man fear? Luck governs all!
There's no foreknowledge, and no providence!
Take life at random. Live as best you can.
That's the best way. What! Fear that you may wed
Your mother? Many a man has dreamt as much,
And so may you! The man who values least
Such scruples, lives his life most easily.   60

OEDIPUS. All this were well enough, that you have said,
Were not my mother living. Though your words
Be true, my mother lives, and I must fear.
JOCASTA. Your father's death at least is a great hope.
OEDIPUS. Yes, but she lives, and I am still afraid.
MESSENGER. What woman is the cause of all these terrors?
OEDIPUS. Merope, sir, that dwelt with Polybus.
MESSENGER. What find you both to fear in Merope?
OEDIPUS. An oracle from the gods, most terrible.
MESSENGER. May it be told, or did the gods forbid?   70
OEDIPUS. No, you may hear it. Phoebus hath said that I
Must come to know my mother's body, come
To shed with my own hand my father's blood.
Therefore I have put Corinth this long time
Far from me. Fortune has been kind, and yet
To see a parent's face is best of all.
MESSENGER. Was this the fear that drove you from your home?

OEDIPUS. This, and my will never to slay my father.
MESSENGER. Then since I only came to serve you, sir,
    Why should I hesitate to end your fear?   80
OEDIPUS. Ah! If you could, you should be well rewarded!
MESSENGER. Why, that was my chief thought in coming here,
    To do myself some good when you come home.
OEDIPUS. No, where my parents are, I'll not return!
MESSENGER. Son, I can see, you know not what you do.
OEDIPUS. 'Fore God, what mean you, sir? Say what you know.
MESSENGER. If this be all that frightens you from home!—
OEDIPUS. All? 'Tis the fear Apollo may prove true—
MESSENGER. And you polluted, and your parents wronged?
OEDIPUS. Aye, it is that, good man! Always that fear!   90
MESSENGER. Can you not see the folly of such fancies?
OEDIPUS. Folly? Why folly, since I am their son?
MESSENGER. Because King Polybus was nothing to you!
OEDIPUS. How now? The father that begot me, nothing?
MESSENGER. No more, no less, than I who speak to you!
OEDIPUS. How should my father rank with naught—with you?
MESSENGER. He never was your father, nor am I.
OEDIPUS. His reason, then, for calling me his son?
MESSENGER. You were a gift. He had you from these arms.
OEDIPUS. He gave that great love to a stranger's child?   100
MESSENGER. Because he had none of his own to love.
OEDIPUS. So. Did you buy this child,—or was it yours?
MESSENGER. I found you where Cithaeron's valleys wind.
OEDIPUS. Our Theban hills! What made you travel here?
MESSENGER. Once on these very hills I kept my flocks.
OEDIPUS. A shepherd? Travelling to earn your wages?
MESSENGER. Yes, but your saviour too, my son, that day!
OEDIPUS. What ailed me, that you found me in distress?
MESSENGER. Ask your own feet. They best can answer that.
OEDIPUS. No, no! Why name that old familiar hurt?   110
MESSENGER. I set you free. Your feet were pinned together!
OEDIPUS. A brand of shame, alas! from infancy!
MESSENGER. And from that fortune comes the name you bear.

OEDIPUS. Who named me? Who? Father or mother? Speak!

MESSENGER. I know not. He that gave you to me—may!

OEDIPUS. You found me not? You had me from another?

MESSENGER. Another shepherd bade me take you. True.

OEDIPUS. What shepherd? Can you tell me? Do you know?

MESSENGER. I think they called him one of Laius' people.

OEDIPUS. Laius? The same that once was King in Thebes?   120

MESSENGER. Aye. 'Twas the same. For him he shepherded.

OEDIPUS. Ah! Could I find him? Is he still alive?

MESSENGER. You best can tell, you, natives of the place!

OEDIPUS. Has any man here present knowledge of
    The shepherd he describes? Has any seen,
    Or here or in the pastures, such an one?
    Speak! It is time for full discovery!

CHORUS. I think, my lord, he means that countryman
    Whose presence you desired. But there is none,
    Perchance, can tell you better than the Queen.   130

OEDIPUS. You heard him, wife. Think you he means the man
    Whom we await already? Was it he?

JOCASTA. What matter what he means? Oh, take no heed,
    And waste no thoughts, I beg you, on such tales.

OEDIPUS. For me it is not possible—to hold
    Such clues as these, and leave my secret so.

JOCASTA. No! By the gods, no; leave it, if you care
    For your own life. I suffer. 'Tis enough.

OEDIPUS. Take heart. *Your* noble blood is safe, although
    I prove thrice bastard, and three times a slave!   140

JOCASTA. Yet, I beseech you, yield, and ask no more.

OEDIPUS. I cannot yield my right to know the truth.

JOCASTA. And yet I speak—I think—but for your good.

OEDIPUS. And this same good, I find, grows tedious.

JOCASTA. Alas! I pray you may not know yourself.

OEDIPUS. Go, someone, fetch the herdsman! Let the Queen
    Enjoy her pride in her fine family!

JOCASTA. O Wretched, Wretched utterly! That name
    I give you, and henceforth no other name!   [*Exit.*

CHORUS. Why went the Queen so swiftly, Oedipus,   150
   As by some anguish moved? Alas! I fear
   Lest from that silence something ill break forth.

OEDIPUS. Break what break will! My will shall be to see
   My origin however mean! For her,
   She is a woman, proud, and woman's pride
   Likes not perhaps a husband humbly got!
     I am Luck's child. Deeming myself her son,
   I shall not be disowned. She lavishes
   Good gifts upon me, she's my nature's mother!
   Her moons, my cousins, watched my littleness   160
   Wax and grow great. I'll not deny my nature
   But be myself and prove my origin.

CHORUS. To-morrow brings full moon!
     All hail, Cithaeron! Hail!
   If there be wit in me, or any prophet-power,
     To-morrow bringeth thee
    Fresh glory. Oedipus the King
    Shall sing thy praise and call thee his!
     His mother and his nurse!
   All Thebes shall dance to thee, and hymn thy hill,   170
   Because it is well pleasing to the King.
   Apollo, hear us! Be this thing thy pleasure too!

    Who is thy mother, child?
    Is it a maid, perchance,
   Of that fair family that grows not old with years,
     Embraced upon the hills
    By roving Pan? Or else a bride
    Of Loxias, who loveth well
     All upland pasturage?
   Did Hermes, or that dweller on the hills,   180
   Bacchus, from one of Helicon's bright Nymphs,
   His chosen playmates, take the child for his delight?

OEDIPUS. If I may guess—I never met the man—
   I think, good friends, yonder I see the herd

Whom we so long have sought. His many years
Confirm it, for they tally with the years
Of this our other witness; and the guides
I know for men of mine. Can *you*, perchance,
Be certain? You have seen, and know the man.
CHORUS. Indeed I know him. Laius trusted him,   190
Though but a shepherd, more than other men.

Enter HERDSMAN

OEDIPUS. This question first to you, Corinthian:—
Is this the man you mean?
MESSENGER.   Aye, this is he.
OEDIPUS. Look hither, sir, and answer everything
That I shall ask. Were you once Laius' man?
HERDSMAN. I was, a house-bred servant, no bought slave!
OEDIPUS. What was your work? What was your way of life?
HERDSMAN. The chief part of my life I kept the flocks.
OEDIPUS. Which were the regions where you camped the most?
HERDSMAN. Cithaeron—or sometimes the country round.   200
OEDIPUS. Ah, then you know this man? You saw him there?
HERDSMAN. I saw him? Saw him when? What man, my lord?
OEDIPUS. Yonder!—Did nothing ever pass between you?
HERDSMAN. No—speaking out of hand, from memory.
MESSENGER. Small wonder he forgets! Come, I'll remind
His ignorance, my lord. I make no doubt
He knows that once around Cithaeron's hills
He tended his two flocks—I had but one—
Yet served for company three summer-times,
The six long months from spring to autumn nights.   210
And when at last the winter came, I drove
Down to my farm, and he to Laius' folds.
Was it so done as I have said, or no?
HERDSMAN. 'Tis very long ago. Yes, it is true.
MESSENGER. Now tell me this:—You know you gave me once
A boy, to rear him as a child of mine?
HERDSMAN. What do you mean? Why do you ask me?

MESSENGER.   Why?

  Because, my friend, that child is now your King!

HERDSMAN. A curse upon you! Silence! Hold your peace.

OEDIPUS. No, no! You must not chide him, sir! 'Tis you   220
  That should be chid, not he, for speaking so.

HERDSMAN. Nay, good my master, what is my offence?

OEDIPUS. This: that you answer nothing—of the child.

HERDSMAN. 'Tis nothing. He knows nothing. 'Tis but talk.

OEDIPUS. You will not speak to please me? Pain shall make you!

HERDSMAN. No! By the gods, hurt me not! I am old.

OEDIPUS. Come, one of you. Quick! Fasten back his arms!

HERDSMAN. O Wretched, Wretched! Why? What would you
  know?

OEDIPUS. Did you, or did you not, give him the child?

HERDSMAN. I gave it him. Would I had died that day.   230

OEDIPUS. This day you shall, unless you speak the truth.

HERDSMAN. Alas! And if I speak, 'tis worse, far worse.

OEDIPUS. Ah! So the fellow means to trifle with us!

HERDSMAN. No, no! I have confessed I gave it him.

OEDIPUS. How came you by it? Was the child your own?

HERDSMAN. It was not mine. Another gave it me.

OEDIPUS. Another? Who, and of what house in Thebes?

HERDSMAN. Nay, for the gods' love, Master, ask no more.

OEDIPUS. Make me repeat my question, and you die!

HERDSMAN. The answer is:—a child of Laius' house.   240

OEDIPUS. Slave born? Or kinsman to the royal blood?

HERDSMAN.   Alas!
  So it has come, the thing I dread to tell.

OEDIPUS. The thing I dread to hear. Yet I must hear it.

HERDSMAN. Thus then:—they said 'twas . . . Laius' son. . . . And
  yet
  Perhaps Jocasta best can answer that.

OEDIPUS. Jocasta gave it you?

HERDSMAN.   She gave it me.

OEDIPUS. For what?

HERDSMAN.   She bade me do away with it.

OEDIPUS. Its mother! Could she?

HERDSMAN.   Fearing prophecies—

OEDIPUS. What prophecies?

HERDSMAN.   His father he must kill!

OEDIPUS. And yet you let this old man take him? Why?   250

HERDSMAN. 'Twas pity, sir. I thought: he dwells afar,
   And takes him to some distant home. But he
   Saved him to suffer! If you are the child
   He saith, no man is more unfortunate.

OEDIPUS. Alas! It comes! It comes! And all is true!
   Light! Let me look my last on thee, for I
   Stand naked now. Shamefully was I born:
   In shame I wedded: to my shame I slew.

                              [*Exeunt all except the Chorus.*

CHORUS. Ah! Generations of mankind!
   Living, I count your life as nothingness.   260
         None hath more of happiness,
         None that mortal is, than this:
         But to seem to be, and then,
              Having seemed, to fail.
      Thine, O unhappy Oedipus,
      Thine is the fatal destiny,
   That bids me call no mortal creature blest.

      Zeus! To the very height of wit
   He shot, and won the prize of perfect life;
         Conqueror that slew the maid,   270
         Who, with crooked claw and tongue
         Riddling, brought us death, when he
              Rose and gave us life.
      That day it was that hailed thee King,
      Preferred above mankind in state
   And honour, Master of the Might of Thebes.

      To-day, alas! no tale so sad as thine!
         No man whom changing life hath lodged

So close with Hell, and all her plagues, and all her sorrowing!
    Woe for the fame of Oedipus!   280
  For the son hath lain where the father lay,
  And the bride of one is the bride of both.
How could the field that the father sowed endure him
    So silently so long?

  Time knoweth all. Spite of thy purposing,
    Time hath discovered thee, to judge
The monstrous mating that defiled the father through the son.
    Woe for the babe that Laius got!
  And I would I never had looked on thee,
  And the songs I sing are a dirge for thee.   290
This is the end of the matter: he that saved me,
    Hath made me desolate.

Enter a MESSENGER *from the Palace*

MESSENGER. Great Lords, that keep the dignities of Thebes,
  What doings must ye hear, what sights must see,
  And oh! what grief must bear, if ye are true
  To Cadmus and the breed of Labdacus!
  Can Ister or can Phasis wash this house—
  I trow not—, with their waters, from the guilt
  It hides? . . . Yet soon shall publish to the light
  Fresh, not unpurposed evil. 'Tis the woe   300
  That we ourselves have compassed, hurts the most.
CHORUS. That which we knew already, was enough
  For lamentation. What have you besides?
MESSENGER. This is the briefest tale for me to tell,
  For you to hear:—your Queen Jocasta's dead.
CHORUS. Alas! Poor lady! Dead! What was the cause?
MESSENGER. She died by her own hand. Of what befell
  The worst is not for you, who saw it not.
  Yet shall you hear, so much as memory
  Remains in me, the sad Queen's tragedy.   310
    When in her passionate agony she passed
  Beyond those portals, straight to her bridal-room

She ran, and ever tore her hair the while;
Clashed fast the doors behind her; and within,
Cried to her husband Laius in the grave,
With mention of that seed whereby he sowed
Death for himself, and left to her a son
To get on her fresh children, shamefully.
So wept she for her bridal's double woe,
Husband of husband got, and child of child.   320
And after that—I know not how—she died.

We could not mark her sorrows to the end,
For, with a shout, Oedipus broke on us,
And all had eyes for him. Hither he rushed
And thither. For a sword he begged, and cried:
'Where is that wife that mothered in one womb
Her husband and his children! Show her me!
No wife of mine!' As thus he raged, some god—
'Twas none of us—guided him where she lay.
And he, as guided, with a terrible shout,   330
Leapt at her double door; free of the bolts
Burst back the yielding bar,—and was within.
And there we saw Jocasta. By a noose
Of swaying cords, caught and entwined, she hung.

He too has seen her—with a moaning cry
Looses the hanging trap, and on the ground
Has laid her. Then—Oh, sight most terrible!—
He snatched the golden brooches from the Queen,
With which her robe was fastened, lifted them,
And struck. Deep to the very founts of sight   340
He smote, and vowed those eyes no more should see
The wrongs he suffered, and the wrong he did.
'Henceforth,' he cried, 'be dark!—since ye have seen
Whom ye should ne'er have seen, and never knew
Them that I longed to find.' So chanted he,
And raised the pins again, and yet again,
And every time struck home. Blood from the eyes
Sprinkled his beard, and still fresh clammy drops

Welled in a shower unceasing, nay, a storm
With blood for rain, and hail of clotting gore.   350
    So from these twain hath evil broken; so
    Are wife and husband mingled in one woe.
Justly their ancient happiness was known
For happiness indeed; and lo! to-day—
Tears and Disasters, Death and Shame, and all
The ills the world hath names for—all are here.
CHORUS. And hath he found some respite now from pain?
MESSENGER. He shouts, and bids open the doors, and show
    To all his Thebes this father-murderer,
    This mother—Leave the word. It is not clean.   360
He would be gone from Thebes, nor stay to see
His home accursèd by the curse he swore;
Yet hath he not the strength. He needs a guide,
Seeing his griefs are more than man can bear.
    Nay, he himself will show you. Look! The gates
Fall open, and the sight that you shall see
Is such that even hate must pity it.

Enter OEDIPUS, *blind*

CHORUS. O sight for all the world to see
    Most terrible! O suffering
Of all mine eyes have seen most terrible!   370
    Alas! What Fury came on thee?
    What evil Spirit, from afar,
    O Oedipus! O wretched!
      Leapt on thee, to destroy?

I cannot even, Alas! look
Upon thy face, though much I have
To ask of thee, and much to hear,
    Aye, and to see—I cannot!
    Such terror is in thee!
OEDIPUS. Alas! O Wretched! Whither go   380
    My steps? My voice? It seems to float
      Far, far away from me.

> Alas! Curse of my Life, how far
>   Thy leap hath carried thee!

CHORUS. To sorrows none can bear to see or hear.

OEDIPUS.   Ah! The cloud!

Visitor unspeakable! Darkness upon me horrible!

Unconquerable! Cloud that may not ever pass away!
                Alas!

And yet again, alas! How deep they stab—   390
These throbbing pains, and all those memories.

CHORUS. Where such afflictions are, I marvel not
If soul and body make one doubled woe.

OEDIPUS.   Ah! My friend!

Still remains thy friendship. Still thine is the help that comforts me,

And kindness, that can look upon these dreadful eyes unchanged.
                Ah me!

My friend, I feel thy presence. Though mine eyes
Be darkened, yet I hear thy voice, and know.   399

CHORUS. Oh, dreadful deed! How wert thou steeled to quench
Thy vision thus? What Spirit came on thee?

OEDIPUS. Apollo! 'Twas Apollo, friends,
Willed the evil, willed, and brought the agony to pass!
        And yet the hand that struck was mine, mine only, wretched.
            Why should I see, whose eyes
        Had no more any good to look upon?

CHORUS. 'Twas even as thou sayest.

OEDIPUS. Aye. For me.—Nothing is left for sight,
            Nor anything to love:
        Nor shall the sound of greetings any more   410
            Fall pleasant on my ear.

Away! Away! Out of the land, away!
        Banishment, banishment! Fatal am I, accursed,
            And the hate on me, as on no man else, of the gods!

CHORUS. Unhappy in thy fortune and the wit
That shows it thee. Would thou hadst never known.

OEDIPUS. A curse upon the hand that loosed
  In the wilderness the cruel fetters of my feet,
    Rescued me, gave me life. Ah! Cruel was his pity,
      Since, had I died, so much   420
    I had not harmed myself and all I love.
CHORUS. Aye, even so 'twere better.
OEDIPUS. Aye, for life never had led me then
      To shed my father's blood;
    Men had not called me husband of the wife
      That bore me in the womb.
  But now—but now.—Godless am I, the son
    Born of impurity, mate of my father's bed,
      And if worse there be, I am Oedipus! It is mine!
CHORUS. In this I know not how to call thee wise,   430
  For better wert thou dead than living—blind.
OEDIPUS. Nay, give me no more counsel. Bid me not
  Believe my deed, thus done, is not well done.
  I know 'tis well. When I had passed the grave,
  How could those eyes have met my father's gaze,
  Or my unhappy mother's—since on both
  I have done wrongs beyond all other wrong?
  Or live and see my children?—Children born
  As they were born! What pleasure in that sight?
  None for these eyes of mine, for ever, none.   440
  Nor in the sight of Thebes, her castles, shrines
  And images of the gods, whereof, alas!
  I robbed myself—myself, I spoke that word,
  I that she bred and nurtured, I her prince,
  And bade her thrust the sinner out, the man
  Proved of the gods polluted—Laius' son.
  When such a stain by my own evidence
  Was on me, could I raise my eyes to them?
  No! Had I means to stop my ears, and choke
  The wells of sound, I had not held my hand,   450
  But closed my body like a prison-house
  To hearing as to sight. Sweet for the mind

To dwell withdrawn, where troubles could not come.
 Cithaeron! Ah, why didst thou welcome me?
Why, when thou hadst me there, didst thou not kill,
Never to show the world myself—my birth?
 O Polybus, and Corinth, and the home
Men called my father's ancient house, what sores
Festered beneath that beauty that ye reared,
Discovered now, sin out of sin begot!   460
 O ye three roads, O secret mountain-glen,
Trees, and a pathway narrowed to the place
Where met the three, do you remember me?
I gave you blood to drink, my father's blood,
And so my own! Do you remember that?
The deed I wrought for you? Then, how I passed
Hither to other deeds?
     O Marriage-bed
That gave me birth, and, having borne me, gave
Fresh children to your seed, and showed the world
Father, son, brother, mingled and confused, 470
Bride, mother, wife in one, and all the shame
Of deeds the foulest ever known to man.
 No. Silence for a deed so ill to do
Is better. Therefore lead me hence, away!
To hide me or to kill. Or to the sea
Cast me, where you shall look on me no more.
Come! Deign to touch me, though I am a man
Accursèd. Yield! Fear nothing! Mine are woes
That no man else, but I alone, must bear. 479
CHORUS. Look, ye who dwell in Thebes. This man was Oedipus.
That Mighty King, who knew the riddle's mystery,
Whom all the city envied, Fortune's favourite.
Behold, in the event, the storm of his calamities,
And, being mortal, think on that last day of death,
Which all must see, and speak of no man's happiness
Till, without sorrow, he hath passed the goal of life.
        [Exeunt omnes.

POINTS FOR DISCUSSION

1. What is the information which the Messenger from Corinth intends to bring to Oedipus, and what is the other information which he is used to convey? There is an amazing contrast between the two—trace the manner in which he is made to pass from one to the other.

2. Why does Jocasta attempt to persuade Oedipus not to summon the Herdsman? What is the effect of her words?

3. What link is there between Jocasta and the Herdsman so far as their dramatic function is concerned? Why is the Herdsman unwilling to speak?

4. 'Line by line' dialogue, or *stichomythia*, like that between Oedipus and the Herdsman, was common in Greek Drama. Why is it used in this passage? What are its disadvantages?

5. What are the dramatic purposes of the speech of the Chorus which follows the wild rush of Oedipus into the Palace?

6. Is there any dramatic justification for the physical horror of the death of Jocasta and the blinding of Oedipus? (A line in one of the speeches of the Chorus after the entry of the blinded Oedipus points to the explanation.)

7. What does the play gain, and what does it lose, by the reporting, instead of the presentation, of the death of Jocasta and the blinding of Oedipus?

8. The great sin of many Greek tragic heroes was a blind over-confidence, called *hubris*. What examples are there of *hubris* in this play?

9. What is the function of the Chorus? Does it enter into the play, like one of the characters, or does it stand apart, like an 'ideal spectator' or commentator? Are its comments always wise?

10. What factors in the plot of the play make it an almost ideal example of Nemesis?

11. '. . . feelings of pity and terror'. How are these conflicting emotions aroused by the play?

12. It is said that drama depends upon conflict. What is the conflict in this play?

CHAPTER II

THE DRAMA OF TWO WORLDS

ALTHOUGH there was little in common between Medieval England and Ancient Greece, the drama of each period is linked by having a common purpose. In Medieval England, as in Ancient Greece, drama had sprung into being as part of a religious festival, as part of an attempt to give fresh significance to stories which were themselves well known in general outline. This is not the place to enter with any detail into the origin of drama in the English Church. Some of the stories of the Bible, particularly the story of the death and resurrection of Christ, were acted in a simple way in the church by the monks, and this acting proved so popular that more and more of the Bible was put into dramatic form. Not content with this, some of the playwrights introduced stories which had no place in the Bible, and the Church refused to allow such plays to be acted in the ecclesiastical buildings. The *Miracle Plays*, as they were called, were then acted outside the church; and developed in a much freer way than was possible for the Greek plays, which continued to the end to be acted within the temple of Dionysus.

At the same time, another kind of drama developed, known as the *Morality Plays*, which are the particular concern of this chapter. The kind of story which interested the Greeks has already been mentioned. The character of the hero was taken for granted, and interest arose from seeing how the life of a great man could end in disaster even though his intentions and motives might be founded on a high endeavour towards what he felt to be a worthy aim. The people in the Middle Ages did not take men for granted, nor did they assume that a man's intentions are always the same.

They became interested not so much in a man's misfortunes as in the causes of those misfortunes. As they were Christians, the idea of Fate or Nemesis (on which the Greeks had relied to account for what they were unable to explain) had become an impossible belief; if a man met with disaster, then some defect in his own character must be the cause. Now a man's character is determined by his thoughts, and it is not easy at first to make up a play which will be chiefly concerned with a man's thoughts. To understand this kind of medieval play, it is necessary to remember that it was an experiment in something new, an attempt to show by means of a play how a man's mind works and how his character is formed.

The method used was very simple. Most people have the experience at some time in their life of feeling that their mind is in two parts, each part urging them to a different course of action. 'The voice of conscience' has become proverbial. The medieval playwrights pretended that these contrary wishes or impulses of the mind were real people, and brought them on to the stage as characters. There were many of them. There were the impulses which drove men towards evil; these were known as the Seven Deadly Sins: Pride, Envy, Sloth, Intemperance, Avarice, Anger, and Lust; and there were the Seven Moral Virtues: Faith, Hope, Charity, Justice, Prudence, Temperance, and Fortitude. All the writers did not have quite the same list, but most of them agreed in showing that man's life was a war between these different influences, a war which went on within him, rather than without.

From another point of view, the plays may be regarded as attempts to show men the events of this life against the background of eternity. They manifest an ever present consciousness of a duality in human experience, a clear-cut division between the world of sense and the world of soul, between the things of the flesh and the things of the spirit.

These two worlds may be kept separate throughout life, but they must draw ever closer together at the approach of death. The most famous of the Morality Plays, *Everyman*, takes as its theme the moments when death is imminent, and shows what a revaluation Everyman has to make of those things in his life which had once seemed all-important.

EVERYMAN

HERE BEGINNETH A TREATISE HOW THE HIGH FATHER OF HEAVEN SENDETH DEATH TO SUMMON EVERY CREATURE TO COME AND GIVE ACCOUNT OF THEIR LIVES IN THIS WORLD AND IS IN MANNER OF A MORAL PLAY.

GOD *speaks from above*

GOD. I perceive here in my majesty,
How that all creatures be to me unkind,
Living without dread in worldly prosperity.
Of ghostly[1] sight the people be so blind,
Drowned in sin, they know me not for their God.
In worldly riches is all their mind,
They fear not my righteousness, the sharp rod;
My law that I shewed when I for them died
They forget clean, and shedding of my blood red;
I hanged between two, it cannot be denied;   10
To get them life I suffered to be dead;
I healed their feet, with thorns hurt was my head.
I could do no more than I did, truly;
And now I see the people do clean forsake me.
They use the seven deadly sins damnable;
As pride, covetise, wrath and lechery
Now in the world be made commendable.
I hoped well that every man
In my glory should make his mansion,

[1] Spiritual.

And thereto I had them all elect;   20
But now I see, like traitors deject,
They thank me not for the pleasure that I to them meant,
Nor yet for their being that I them have lent.
I proffered the people great multitude of mercy,
And few there be that asketh it heartily;
They be so cumbered with worldly riches,
That needs on them I must do justice,
On every man living without fear.
Where art thou, Death, thou mighty messenger?

Enter DEATH

DEATH. Almighty God, I am here at your will,   30
    Your commandment to fulfil.
GOD. Go thou to Everyman,
    And show him, in my name,
    A pilgrimage he must on him take,
    Which he in no wise may escape;
    And that he bring with him a sure reckoning
    Without delay or any tarrying.

                            [GOD *withdraws.*

DEATH. Lord, I will in the world go run over all,
    And cruelly outsearch both great and small;
    Every man will I beset that liveth beastly   40
    Out of God's laws, and dreadeth not folly:
    He that loveth riches I will strike with my dart,
    His sight to blind, and from heaven to depart,
    Except that alms be his good friend,
    In hell for to dwell, world without end.

Enter EVERYMAN *at a distance*

Lo, yonder I see Everyman walking;
Full little he thinketh on my coming;
His mind is on fleshly lusts and his treasure,
And great pain it shall cause him to endure
Before the Lord, Heaven's King.   50

C

Everyman, stand still! Whither art thou going
Thus gaily? Hast thou thy Maker forgot?

EVERYMAN. Full unready I am such reckoning to give.
I know thee not: what messenger art thou?

DEATH. I am Death, that no man dreadeth;
For every man I rest, and no man spareth;
For it is God's commandment
That all to me should be obedient.

EVERYMAN. O Death, thou comest when I had thee least in
mind;
In thy power it lieth me to save, 60
Yet of my good will I give thee, if ye will be kind,
Yea, a thousand pound shalt thou have,
If thou defer this matter till another day.

DEATH. Everyman, it may not be by no way;
I set not by gold, silver, nor riches,
Ne by pope, emperor, king, duke, ne princes.
For, if I would receive gifts great,
All the world I might get;
But my custom is clean contrary.
I give thee no respite: come hence, and not tarry! 70

EVERYMAN. Alas, shall I have no longer respite?
I may say Death giveth no warning:
To think on thee, it maketh my heart sick,
For all unready is my book of reckoning.
But twelve year and I might have abiding,
My counting-book I would make so clear,
That my reckoning I should not need to fear.
Wherefore, Death, I pray thee, for God's mercy,
Spare me till I be provided of remedy!

DEATH. Thee availeth not to cry, weep, and pray: 80
But haste thee lightly that thou wert gone that journey,
And prove thy friends if thou can.
For, wete thou well, the tide abideth no man;
And in the world each living creature
For Adam's sin must die of nature.

EVERYMAN. Death, if I should this pilgrimage take,
   And my reckoning surely make,
   Show me, for saint charity,
   Should I not come again shortly?

DEATH. No, Everyman; and thou be once there,   90
   Thou mayst never more come here,
   Trust me verily.

EVERYMAN. O gracious God, in the high seat celestial,
   Have mercy on me in this most need!
   Shall I have no company from this vale terrestrial
   Of mine acquaintance that way me to lead?

DEATH. Yea, if any be so hardy,
   That would go with thee and bear thee company.
   Hie thee that thou wert gone to God's magnificence,
   Thy reckoning to give before his presence.   100
   What! weenest thou thy life is given thee,
   And thy worldly goods also?

EVERYMAN. I had weened so, verily.

DEATH. Nay, nay; it was but lent thee;
   For as soon as thou art go,
   Another awhile shall have it, and then go therefro
   Even as thou hast done.
   Everyman, thou art mad; thou hast thy wits five.
   And here on earth will not amend thy life,
   For suddenly I do come.   110

EVERYMAN. O wretched caitiff! whither shall I flee
   That I might scape this endless sorrow?
   Now, gentle Death, spare me till to-morrow,
   That I may amend me
   With good advisement.

DEATH. Nay, thereto I will not consent,
   Nor no man will I respite,
   But to the heart suddenly I shall smite
   Without any advisement.
   And now out of thy sight I will me hie;   120
   See thou make thee ready shortly,

For thou mayst say this is the day
That no man living may scape away.   [*Exit* DEATH.

EVERYMAN. Alas! I may well weep with sighs deep;
    Now have I no manner of company
    To help me in my journey, and me to keep;
    And also my writing is full unready.
    How shall I do now for to excuse me?
    I would to God I had never be gete![1]
    To my soul a full great profit it had be;   130
    For now I fear pains huge and great.
    The time passeth. Lord, help, that all wrought!
    For though I mourn it availeth nought.
    The day passeth, and is almost a-go;
    I wot not well what for to do.
    To whom were I best my complaint to make?
    What if I to Fellowship thereof spake,
    And showed him of this sudden chance?
    For in him is all mine affiance;[2]
    We have in the world so many a day   140
    Been good friends in sport and play.
    I see him yonder, certainly;
    I trust that he will bear me company;
    Therefore to him will I speak to ease my sorrow.
    Well met, good Fellowship, and good morrow!

FELLOWSHIP *speaketh*

FELLOWSHIP. Everyman, good morrow, by this day!
    Sir, why lookest thou so piteously?
    If any thing be amiss, I pray thee, me say,
    That I may help to remedy.

EVERYMAN. Yea, good Fellowship, yea,   150
    I am in great jeopardy.

FELLOWSHIP. My true friend, show to me your mind;
    I will not forsake thee, to my life's end,
    In the way of good company.

        [1] Been born.   [2] Trust.

EVERYMAN. Ye speak like a good friend; I believe you well;
    I shall deserve it, and I may.
FELLOWSHIP. I speak of no deserving, by this day!
    For he that will say, and nothing do,
    Is not worthy with good company to go.
    Therefore show me the grief of your mind,   160
    As to your friend most loving and kind.
EVERYMAN. I shall show you how it is;
    Commanded I am to go a journey,
    A long way, hard and dangerous,
    And give a strait count, without delay,
    Before the high judge, Adonai.
    Wherefore, I pray you, bear me company,
    As ye have promised, in this journey.
FELLOWSHIP. That is matter indeed! Promise is duty,
    But, if I should take such a voyage on me,   170
    I know it well, it should be to my pain:
    Also it maketh me afeard, certain.
    But let us take counsel here as well as we can,
    For your words would fear a strong man.
EVERYMAN. Why, ye said, if I had need,
    Ye would me never forsake, quick ne dead,
    Though it were to hell, truly.
FELLOWSHIP. So I said, certainly,
    But such pleasures be set aside, thee sooth to say:
    And also, if we took such a journey,   180
    When should we come again?
EVERYMAN. Nay, never again till the day of doom!
FELLOWSHIP. In faith, then will not I come there!
    Who hath you these tidings brought?
EVERYMAN. Indeed, Death was with me here.
FELLOWSHIP. Now, by God that all hath bought,
    If Death were the messenger,
    For no man that is living to-day
    I will not go that loath journey—
    Not for the father that begat me!   190

EVERYMAN. Ye promised other wise, pardie.

FELLOWSHIP. I wot well I said so, truly;
    And yet if thou wilt eat, and drink, and make good cheer,
    I would not forsake you, while the day is clear,
    Trust me, verily!

EVERYMAN. Yea, thereto ye would be ready!
    To go to mirth, solace, and play
    Your mind will sooner apply
    Than to bear me company in my long journey.

FELLOWSHIP. Now, in good faith, I will not that way.   200
    But if thou wilt murder, or any man kill,
    In that I will help thee with a good will!

EVERYMAN. O that is a simple advice indeed!
    Gentle Fellowship, help me in my necessity!
    We have loved long, and now I need;
    And now, gentle Fellowship, remember me!

FELLOWSHIP. Whether ye have loved me or no,
    By Saint John I will not with thee go!

EVERYMAN. Yet I pray thee, take the labour, and do so much for
    me
    To bring me forward, for saint charity,   210
    And comfort me till I come without the town.

FELLOWSHIP. Nay, if thou would give me a new gown,
    I will not a foot with thee go!
    But if you had tarried, I would not have left thee so.
    And as now, God speed thee in thy journey,
    For from thee I will depart as fast as I may.

EVERYMAN. Whither away, Fellowship? will you forsake me?

FELLOWSHIP. Yea, by my fay! to God I betake thee.

EVERYMAN. Farewell, good Fellowship; for ye my heart is sore;
    Adieu for ever, I shall see thee no more.   220

FELLOWSHIP. In faith, Everyman, farewell now at the end;
    For you I will remember that parting is mourning.

                                              [*Exit* FELLOWSHIP.

EVERYMAN. It is said, in prosperity men friends may find,
    Which in adversity be full unkind.

Now whither for succour shall I flee,
Sith that Fellowship hath forsaken me?
To my kinsmen I will, truly,
Praying them to help me in my necessity;
I believe that they will do so,
For kind will creep where it may not go.[1]   230
I will go say,[2] for yonder I see them go.

> [*His* KINDRED *behave as did* FELLOWSHIP. *They make
> extravagant promises which they are unwilling to carry
> out when they hear that it is* DEATH *who has summoned*
> EVERYMAN.]

Ah, Jesus! is all come hereto?
Lo, fair words maketh fools fain;
They promise and nothing will do certain.
My kinsmen promised me faithfully
For to abide with me steadfastly,
And now fast away do they flee:
Even so Fellowship promised me.
What friend were best me of to provide?
I lose my time here longer to abide.   240
Yet in my mind a thing there is;—
All my life I have loved riches;
If that my Good now help me might,
He would make my heart full light.
I will speak to him in this distress.—
Where art thou, my Goods and riches?
GOODS [*within*]. Who calleth me? Everyman? what haste thou hast!
I lie here in corners, trussed and piled so high,
And in chests I am locked so fast,
Also sacked in bags, thou mayst see with thine eye,   250
I cannot stir; in packs low I lie.
What would ye have? lightly me say.
EVERYMAN. Come hither, Good, in all the haste thou may,
For of counsel I must desire thee.

---

[1] Walk.   [2] Assay, put it to the test.

Enter GOODS

GOODS. Sir, if ye in the world have sorrow or adversity,
  That can I help you to remedy shortly.
EVERYMAN. It is another disease that grieveth me;
  In this world it is not, I tell thee so.
  I am sent for another way to go,
  To give a straight count general   260
  Before the highest Jupiter of all;
  And all my life I have had joy and pleasure in thee,
  Therefore, I pray thee, go with me;
  For, peradventure, thou mayst before God Almighty
  My reckoning help to clean and purify;
  For it is said ever among,
  That money maketh all right that is wrong.
GOODS. Nay, Everyman, I sing another song,
  I follow no man in such voyages;
  For if I went with thee   270
  Thou shouldst fare much the worse for me;
  For because on me thou did set thy mind,
  Thy reckoning I have made blotted and blind,
  That thine account thou cannot make truly;
  And that hast thou for the love of me!
EVERYMAN. That would grieve me full sore,
  When I should come to that fearful answer.
  Up, let us go thither together.
GOODS. Nay, not so, I am too brittle, I may not endure;
  I will follow no man one foot, be ye sure.   280
EVERYMAN. Alas, I have thee loved, and had great pleasure
  All my life-days on good and treasure.
GOODS. That is to thy damnation, without lesing![1]
  For my love is contrary to the love everlasting.
  But if thou had me loved moderately during,
  As, to the poor give part of me,
  Then shouldst thou not in this dolour be,
  Nor in this great sorrow and care.

[1] Lying.

EVERYMAN. Lo, now was I deceived or[1] I was ware,
 And all, I may wit, mis-spending of time.[2]   290
GOODS. What! weenest thou that I am thine?
EVERYMAN. I had weened so.
GOODS. Nay, Everyman, I say no;
 As for a while I was lent thee,
 A season thou hast had me in prosperity.
 My condition is man's soul to kill;
 If I save one, a thousand I do spill.
 Weenest thou that I will follow thee
 From this world? Nay, verily!
EVERYMAN. I had weened otherwise.   300
GOODS. Therefore to thy soul Good is a thief;
 For when thou art dead, this is my guise—
 Another to deceive in this same wise
 As I have done thee, and all to his soul's reprief.
EVERYMAN. O false Good, cursed thou be!
 Thou traitor to God, that hast deceived me,
 And caught me in thy snare!
GOODS. Marry, thou brought thyself in care,
 Whereof I am right glad;
 I must needs laugh, I cannot be sad.   310
EVERYMAN. Ah, Good, thou hast had long my heartly love;
 I gave thee that which should be the Lord's above.
 But wilt thou not go with me in deed?
 I pray thee truth to say.
GOODS. No, so God me speed!
 Therefore farewell, and have good day!   [*Exit* GOODS.
EVERYMAN. O, to whom shall I make my moan
 For to go with me in that heavy journey?
 First Fellowship said he would with me gone;
 His words were very pleasant and gay,   320
 But afterwards he left me alone.
 Then spake I to my kinsmen all in despair,
 And also they gave me words fair,

[1] Before. [2] I can understand that all my time has been mis-spent.

They lacked no fair speaking!
But all forsook me in the ending.
Then went I to my Goods, that I loved best,
In hope to have comfort, but there had I least;
For my Goods sharply did me tell
That he bringeth many into hell.
Then of myself I was ashamed,   330
And so I am worthy to be blamed;
Thus may I well myself hate.
Of whom shall I now counsel take?
I think that I shall never speed
Till that I go to my Good-Deed,
But alas, she is so weak,
That she can neither go nor speak;
Yet will I venture on her now.—
My Good-Deeds, where be you?

          [GOOD-DEEDS *speaks up from the ground.*

GOOD-DEEDS. Here I lie, cold in the ground;   340
  Thy sins hath me sore bound,
  That I cannot stir.

EVERYMAN. O, Good-Deeds, I stand in fear;
  I must you pray of counsel,
  For help now should come right well.

GOOD-DEEDS. Everyman, I have understanding
  That ye be summoned account to make
  Before Messias, of Jerusalem King;
  If you do by me,[1] that journey with you will I take.

EVERYMAN. Therefore I come to you, my moan to make;   350
  I pray you, that ye will go with me.

GOOD-DEEDS. I would full fain, but I cannot stand, verily.

EVERYMAN. Why, is there anything on you fall?

GOOD-DEEDS. Yea, sir, I may thank you of all!
  If ye had perfectly cheered me,
  Your book of account now full ready had be.

          [GOOD-DEEDS *shows him his book of account.*

        [1] If you will follow my advice.

Look, the books of your works and deeds eke;
Behold, how they lie under the feet,
To your soul's heaviness.

EVERYMAN. Our Lord Jesus, help me! 360
For one letter here I can not see.

GOOD-DEEDS. There is a blind reckoning in time of distress!

EVERYMAN. Good-Deeds, I pray you, help me in this need,
Or else I am for ever damned indeed;
Therefore help me to make my reckoning
Before the Redeemer of all thing,
That King is, and was, and ever shall.

GOOD-DEEDS. Everyman, I am sorry of your fall,
And fain would I help you, if I were able.

EVERYMAN. Good-Deeds, your counsel I pray you give me. 370

GOOD-DEEDS. That shall I do verily;
Though that on my feet I may not go,
I have a sister, that shall with you also,
Called Knowledge, which shall with you abide,
To help you to make that dreadful reckoning.

Enter KNOWLEDGE

KNOWLEDGE. Everyman, I will go with thee, and be thy guide,
In thy most need to go by thy side.

EVERYMAN. In good condition I am now in every thing,
And am wholly content with this good thing;
Thanked be God my Creator! 380

KNOWLEDGE. Now go we together lovingly
To Confession, that cleansing river.

EVERYMAN. For joy I weep! I would we were there!
But, I pray you, give me cognition
Where dwelleth that holy man, Confession.

KNOWLEDGE. In the house of salvation:
We shall find him in that place,
That shall us comfort by God's grace.

[KNOWLEDGE *leads* EVERYMAN *to* CONFESSION.

Lo, this is Confession; kneel down and ask mercy,
For he is in good conceit with God Almighty.   390

EVERYMAN. O glorious fountain that all uncleanness doth cla-
    rify,
Wash from me the spots of vice unclean,
That on me no sin may be seen;
I come with Knowledge for my redemption,
Redempt with hearty and full contrition;
For I am commanded a pilgrimage to take,
And great accounts before God to make.
Now I pray you, Shrift, mother of salvation,
Help my Good-Deeds for my piteous exclamation.

CONFESSION. I know your sorrow well, Everyman;   400
Because with Knowledge ye come to me,
I will you comfort as well as I can,
And a precious jewel I will give thee,
Called penance, voider of adversity;
Therewith shall your body chastised be
With abstinence, and perseverance in God's service.

EVERYMAN. Knowledge, give me the scourge of penance;
My flesh therewith shall give a quittance:
I will now begin, if God give me grace.

                    [KNOWLEDGE *gives* EVERYMAN *a scourge.*

KNOWLEDGE. Everyman, God give you time and space: 410
Thus I bequeath you in the hands of our Saviour,
Now may you make your reckoning sure.

EVERYMAN. In the name of the Holy Trinity,
My body sore punished shall be:

                    [*He begins to scourge himself.*

Take this, body, for the sin of the flesh!
Also thou delightest to go gay and fresh,
And in the way of damnation thou did me bring;
Therefore suffer now strokes and punishing!
Now of penance I will wade the water clear,
To save me from purgatory, that sharp fire.   420

                    [GOOD-DEEDS *rises from the floor.*

GOOD-DEEDS. I thank God, now I can walk and go;
 And am delivered of my sickness and woe.
 Therefore with Everyman I will go, and not spare;
 His good works I will help him to declare.
KNOWLEDGE. Be no more sad, but ever rejoice,
 God seeth thy living in his throne above.
 Put on this garment to thy behove,
 Which is wet with your tears,
 Or else before God you may it miss,
 When you to your journey's end come shall.   430
EVERYMAN. Gentle Knowledge, what do you it call?
KNOWLEDGE. It is the garment of sorrow:
 From pain it will you borrow;
 Contrition it is,
 That getteth forgiveness;
 It pleaseth God passing well.
GOOD-DEEDS. Everyman, will you wear it for your heal?
     [EVERYMAN *puts on the robe of contrition.*
EVERYMAN. Now blessed be Jesu, Mary's Son!
 For now have I on true contrition.
 And let us go now without tarrying;   440
 Good-Deeds, have we clear our reckoning?
GOOD-DEEDS. Yea, indeed, I have it here.
EVERYMAN. Then I trust we need not fear.
 Now, friends, let us not part in twain.
KNOWLEDGE. Nay, Everyman, that will we not, certain.
GOOD-DEEDS. Yet must thou lead with thee
 Three persons of great might.
EVERYMAN. Who should they be?
GOOD-DEEDS. Discretion and Strength they hight,[1]
 And thy Beauty may not abide behind.   450
KNOWLEDGE. Also ye must call to mind
 Your Five-wits as for your counsellors.
GOOD-DEEDS. You must have them ready at all hours.
EVERYMAN. How shall I get them hither?
      [1] Are called.

KNOWLEDGE. You must call them all together,
　And they will hear you incontinent.
EVERYMAN. My friends, come hither and be present,
　Discretion, Strength, my Five-wits, and Beauty.

Enter DISCRETION, STRENGTH, FIVE-WITS, *and* BEAUTY

BEAUTY. Here at your will we be all ready.
　What will ye that we should do?　　　　　　　　460
GOOD-DEEDS. That ye would with Everyman go,
　And help him in his pilgrimage.
　Advise you, will ye with him or not in that voyage?
STRENGTH. We will bring him all thither,
　To his help and comfort, ye may believe me.
DISCRETION. So will we go with him all together.
EVERYMAN. Almighty God, loved may thou be!
　I give thee laud that I have hither brought
　Strength, Discretion, Beauty, and Five-Wits; lack I naught;
　And my Good-Deeds, with Knowledge clear,　　　　470
　All be in company at my will here;
　I desire no more to my business.
STRENGTH. And I, Strength, will by you stand in distress,
　Though thou would in battle fight on the ground.
FIVE-WITS. And though it were through the world round,
　We will not depart for sweet nor sour.
BEAUTY. No more will I, unto death's hour,
　Whatsoever thereof befall.
EVERYMAN. Now Jesu be your alder speed.[1]
　I have received the sacrament for my redemption,　　480
　And then mine extreme unction:
　Blessed be all they that counselled me to take it!
　And now, friends, let us go without longer respite:
　I thank God that ye have tarried so long.
　Now set each of you on this rod your hand,
　And shortly follow me:
　I go before, there I would be. God be our guide!
　　　　　　　　[1] May Jesus help you all.

STRENGTH. Everyman, we will not from you go
 Till ye have done this voyage long.
DISCRETION. I, Discretion, will bide by you also.   490
KNOWLEDGE. And though this pilgrimage be never so strong,
 I will never part you fro:
 Everyman, I will be as sure by thee
 As ever I did by Judas Maccabee.
EVERYMAN. Alas, I am so faint I may not stand,
 My limbs under me do fold.
 Friends, let us not turn again to this land,
 Not for all the world's gold;
 For into this cave must I creep
 And turn to the earth, and there to sleep.   500
BEAUTY. What! into this grave? alas!
EVERYMAN. Yea, there shall you consume, more and less.
BEAUTY. And what! should I smother here?
EVERYMAN. Yea, by my faith, and never more appear.
 In this world live no more we shall,
 But in heaven before the highest Lord of all.
BEAUTY. I cross out all this! adieu by Saint John!
 I take my cap in my lap and am gone.
EVERYMAN. What, Beauty, whither will ye?
BEAUTY. Peace, I am deaf; I look not behind me,   510
 Not if thou would give me all the gold in thy chest!

          [*Exit* BEAUTY.

EVERYMAN. Alas, whereto may I trust?
 Beauty goeth fast away from me;
 She promised with me to live and die.
STRENGTH. Everyman, I will thee also forsake and deny;
 Thy game liketh me not at all.
EVERYMAN. Why, then ye will forsake me all?
 Sweet Strength, tarry a little space.
STRENGTH. Nay, sir, by the rood of grace
 I will hie me from thee fast,   520
 Though thou weep till thy heart brast.[1]

       [1] Burst.

EVERYMAN. Ye would ever bide by me, ye said.

STRENGTH. Yea, I have you far enough conveyed;
  Ye be old enough, I understand,
  Your pilgrimage to take on hand;
  I repent me that I hither came.

EVERYMAN. Strength, you to displease I am to blame;
  Yet promise is debt, this ye well wot.

STRENGTH. In faith, I care not!
  Thou art but a fool to complain;   530
  You spend your speech and waste your brain;
  Go thrust thee into the ground!   [*Exit* STRENGTH.

EVERYMAN. I had weened surer I should you have found.
  He that trusteth in his Strength
  She him deceiveth at the length.
  Both Strength and Beauty forsaketh me,
  Yet they promised me fair and lovingly.

DISCRETION. Everyman, I will after Strength be gone;
  As for me, I will leave you alone.

EVERYMAN. Why, Discretion! will ye forsake me?   540

DISCRETION. Yea, in faith, I will go from thee,
  For when Strength goeth before
  I follow after evermore.

EVERYMAN. Yet, I pray thee, for the love of the Trinity,
  Look in my grave once piteously.

DISCRETION. Nay, so nigh will I not come.
  Farewell, every one!   [*Exit* DISCRETION.

EVERYMAN. O all thing faileth, save God alone;
  Beauty, Strength, and Discretion;
  For when Death bloweth his blast,   550
  They all run from me full fast.

FIVE-WITS. Everyman, my leave now of thee I take;
  I will follow the other, for here I thee forsake.

EVERYMAN. Alas! then may I wail and weep,
  For I took you for my best friend.

FIVE-WITS. I will no longer thee keep;
  Now farewell, and there an end!   [*Exit* FIVE-WITS.

EVERYMAN. O Jesu, help, all hath forsaken me!

GOOD-DEEDS. Nay, Everyman, I will bide with thee,
　　I will not forsake thee indeed; 560
　　Thou shalt find me a good friend at need.

EVERYMAN. Gramercy, Good-Deeds; now may I true friends
　　　　see;
　　They have forsaken me, every one;
　　I loved them better than my Good-Deeds alone.
　　Knowledge, will ye forsake me also?

KNOWLEDGE. Yea, Everyman, when ye to death shall go:
　　But not yet, for no manner of danger.

EVERYMAN. Gramercy, Knowledge, with all my heart.

KNOWLEDGE. Nay, yet I will not from hence depart
　　Till I see where ye shall be come. 570

EVERYMAN. Methinketh, alas, that I must be gone
　　To make my reckoning, and my debts pay;
　　For I see my time is nigh spent away.
　　Take example, all ye that this do hear or see,
　　How they that I loved best do forsake me,
　　Except my Good-Deeds that bideth truly.

GOOD-DEEDS. All earthly things is but vanity:
　　Beauty, Strength, and Discretion, do man forsake,
　　Foolish friends and kinsmen, that fair spake,
　　All fleeth save Good-Deeds, and that am I. 580

EVERYMAN. Have mercy on me, God most mighty;
　　And stand by me, thou Mother and Maid, holy Mary!

GOOD-DEEDS. Fear not, I will speak for thee.

EVERYMAN. Here I cry God mercy.

GOOD-DEEDS. Short our end, and minish our pain;
　　Let us go and never come again.

EVERYMAN. Into thy hands, Lord, my soul I commend;
　　Receive it, Lord, that it be not lost;
　　As thou me boughtest, so me defend,
　　And save me from the fiend's boast, 590
　　That I may appear with that blessed host
　　That shall be saved at the day of doom.

D

In manus tuas—of might's most

For ever—*commendo spiritum meum.*

> [EVERYMAN *and* GOOD-DEEDS *descend into the grave.*

KNOWLEDGE. Now hath he suffered that we all shall endure;

The Good-Deeds shall make all sure.

Now hath he made ending.

Methinketh that I hear angels sing,

And make great joy and melody

Where Everyman's soul received shall be.   600

ANGEL [*within*]. Come, excellent elect spouse to Jesu!

Hereabove thou shalt go

Because of thy singular virtue.

Now the soul is taken the body fro;

Thy reckoning is crystal-clear.

Now shalt thou into the heavenly sphere,

Unto the which all ye shall come

That liveth well before the day of doom.

POINTS FOR DISCUSSION

1. The play opens with a speech by God which has often been praised for its high dignity, yet God never appears again in the play. Is this a dramatic defect?

2. What is the dramatic effectiveness of Everyman's offer of a bribe to Death?

3. In the speech by Death in l. 66, would the catalogue *pope, emperor,* &c., be more effective if arranged as a climax?

4. How has Death been represented in literature? What are his chief characteristics in this play? (It may be of interest to compare the dialogue between God and Death with the scenes between God and Satan in the Book of Job, i. 6–12; ii. 1–6.)

5. From time to time in the play, there are general statements about the significance of death. Find some of these, and say whether they are integral parts of the play, or whether they are merely passages thrust into the dialogue for the sake of their moral purpose.

6. Is there any reason why Everyman should expect help from Goods when he has already been disappointed by Fellowship and Kindred?

7. Why is it almost inevitable that there should be many examples of dramatic irony in the play? Which examples are the most effective?

8. Make a study of the play by drawing a simple graph of the plot. The horizontal axis should represent the passage of time (marked by the incidents in the play), and the vertical axis the degree of hopefulness of Everyman.

9. What are the qualities in *Everyman* which have made it of permanent dramatic interest?—it is still occasionally acted on the stage.

10. Could the author of *Everyman* be described as a puritan? What seems to have been his conception of the good life?

CHAPTER III

THE DRAMA OF HUMAN GREATNESS

THE simplicity of the Morality Plays, with their rather clumsy personifications, later developed into something infinitely more complex. A Morality Play was like a dramatized allegory, but in the Elizabethan Age plays began to be written which represented real life. These plays could be as varied as life itself, and it is impossible to say exactly what the audience expected when they sat in the theatre in the mood of 'Let's pretend'. It is impossible to say exactly and fully, but one or two things can be noted.

The most obvious fact about an Elizabethan audience was that they were much more prepared than a modern audience to use their imaginations; and they seem to have enjoyed using their imaginations to an extent which we find it difficult to understand. In one way, this was necessary. The theatre as a building which should exist as a permanent home of dramatic entertainment had not long been in existence, and it had by no means been perfected. Most of the spectators were quite close to the stage, for the area of the theatre was hardly that of a modern tennis court. The stage jutted out into the middle of the building, with the audience (either sitting in galleries or standing) round three sides of it. Some even sat on the stage itself. The lighting was that of the sun, which could shine directly into the theatre, because only the galleries themselves and part of the stage were covered by a roof; all the middle of the building was open to the sky.

At the back of the main stage there was a smaller rear stage which could be curtained off. This was used particularly for indoor scenes, and those which required properties.

But apart from this there was no curtain, and without a curtain there could be no scenery, as there was no opportunity to change it. The lack of scenery was in part compensated for by the use of elaborate and expensive costumes which filled the stage with colour. These costumes were not 'in period': whether the actor took the part of a Roman general or a medieval knight, whether he was the Shah of Persia or the King of England, his costume was that of an Elizabethan gentleman. And finally, both Helen of Troy and Cleopatra of Egypt were acted, not by the beauties of the Elizabethan Age, but by boys young enough to have unbroken voices.

The absence of scenery encouraged the dramatists to disregard the setting, and there are many scenes in Elizabethan plays in which the locality does not matter. When the background became of importance the audience had to create it in their imaginations, transmuting the bare boards of the theatre into the forest of Arden, or putting a veil between themselves and the bright rays of the afternoon sun to make the darkness of the night in which Macbeth murdered Duncan. The dramatist helped them as much as he could in the dialogue, and the absence of scenery has brought into being some passages of exquisite description.

All this left much to the imagination, and it is to the lasting glory of the Elizabethans that their imagination was equal to the demands made upon it. Instead of having their attention distracted by pasteboard castles and painted skies, the audience saw the whole of life through the personality of the characters to whom they were listening. In a modern play the audience are often encouraged to be lazy. What they see before them represents so accurately the scene of the play which they are to witness that they hardly need to imagine anything: the scenery, the properties, the lighting, the dresses—all represent exactly what is required by the play. There is a clear-cut line between the audience and the actors which is drawn at the proscenium and the footlights. The world of the stage is a world of its own, and it is easy for a member of the audience to 'suspend disbelief' for a moment, and to allow himself to think that the people on the stage are in fact the people whom they are supposed to represent. He is watching something which is quite apart and independent.

For an Elizabethan it was different. He might be near or on the stage, as near to the actors as they were to each other. Instead of watching a world apart, he rather became part of a new world, and identified himself with the thoughts, passions, and speeches of the characters whom he was watching. A character could pour out his thoughts in a soliloquy and hold the audience spellbound, because each one of them felt in some measure that those were his words, and that he had suddenly been gifted with the power to express himself in that passage of magnificent poetry to which he was listening. His whole being was enlarged and exalted. The actor could see the audience as distinctly as he could see his fellow actors, and those who were nearest to him were the poorer, and therefore the more openly responsive, members of the audience. It is the reserved and often supercilious occupants of expensive seats in the stalls who are nearest to a modern actor, but the Elizabethan actor was surrounded by the eager, tense faces of an excitable crowd who reflected his every emotion. Instead of actors and audience, there was a theatre of people, a unity.

As a result of this unity a new interest became possible in drama. Greek audiences were always divided from the characters in the plays which they were watching by what may be called the line of knowledge. The audience knew the end of the story, and although they might share the emotions of the characters in a tragedy they could never share their thoughts, because the audience knew all the time that those thoughts were mistaken. The interest of the plays was the conflict between man and the forces outside him threatening his destruction. An Elizabethan audience did not know the end of the story, and they were able to share the thoughts as well as the emotions of the characters. It was not the conflict between man and the forces outside him which became the chief interest of the play, but the conflict within the mind of man between the forces which are the springs of human action.

It has already been noticed that, even in the early simple Morality Plays, this interest had been present in the personifications of virtues and vices; and at the time of the Elizabethan drama this interest achieved a new mode of expression through a group of dramatists who came to be known as the University Wits. Robert Greene, John Lyly, Thomas Kyd, and Christopher Marlowe were the best-known names among them. Most of these playwrights had a university education which brought them into contact with the classical tragedies of the kind mentioned in Chapter I, and their great achievement was to give to the strivings within the mind of man an expression as tremendous as that which the Classical dramatists had given to the strivings of man against Fate.

Among the University Wits the greatest advance was made by Christopher Marlowe. He was influenced by the Classics, not merely through dramas, but through the contribution which was made by Classical literature and learning to that movement of the spirit in Europe which has come to be called the Renaissance. In every direction the frontiers of human knowledge were being advanced; ordered systems, centuries old, were being transformed. Man went out over the sea and discovered continents so great in their extent

that they were called the New World. With the telescope
he lessened the distances to the stars and brought in a new
universe. In Germany and England he asserted his right
to dispense with the mediation of the Church, and by faith
to justify himself in the sight of God. It seemed as if there
could be no end to human greatness. There were moments
when God Himself was unnecessary, and it was possible to say

> I count religion but a childish toy,
> And hold there is no sin but ignorance.

Such moments pass. Like the *hubris* of the Classical heroes,
they bring a retribution as crushing as their exaltation has
been overweening. Both Marlowe and Shakespeare wrote
plays on human ambition, and both concentrated attention
upon the greatness of the man, rather than upon the greatness
of his overthrow. Marlowe took as his theme the legend of
Faustus, the man who bartered his soul for earthly dominion,
while Shakespeare borrowed a tale from the *Chronicles* of
Holinshed.

THE TRAGICAL HISTORY OF DOCTOR FAUSTUS

By CHRISTOPHER MARLOWE

SCENE I

FAUSTUS *discovered in his study*

FAUSTUS. Settle thy studies, Faustus, and begin
  To sound the depth of that thou wilt profess:
  Having commenc'd, be a divine in show,
  Yet level at the end of every art,
  And live and die in Aristotle's works.
  Sweet Analytics, 'tis thou hast ravish'd me!   [*Reads.*
  Bene disserere est finis logices.
  Is, to dispute well, logic's chiefest end?
  Affords this art no greater miracle?

Then read no more; thou hast attain'd that end: 10
A greater subject fitteth Faustus' wit:
Bid Economy farewell, and Galen come,
Seeing, *Ubi desinit philosophus, ibi incipit medicus*:
Be a physician, Faustus; heap up gold,
And be eternis'd for some wondrous cure: [*Reads.*
Summum bonum medicinae sanitas,
The end of physic is our body's health.
Why, Faustus, hast thou not attain'd that end?
Is not thy common talk found aphorisms?
Are not thy bills hung up as monuments,   20
Whereby whole cities have escap'd the plague,
And thousand desperate maladies been eas'd?
Yet art thou still but Faustus, and a man.
Couldst thou make men to live eternally,
Or, being dead, raise them to life again,
Then this profession were to be esteem'd.
Physic, farewell! Where is Justinian?   [*Reads.*
Si una eademque res legatur duobus, alter rem, alter valorem,
   rei, etc.
A pretty case of paltry legacies!   [*Reads.*
Exhaereditare filium non potest pater, nisi, etc.   30
Such is the subject of the institute,
And universal body of the law:
This study fits a mercenary drudge,
Who aims at nothing but external trash;
Too servile and illiberal for me.
When all is done, divinity is best:
Jerome's Bible, Faustus; view it well.   [*Reads.*
Stipendium peccati mors est. Ha! *Stipendium, etc.*
The reward of sin is death: that's hard.   [*Reads.*
Si peccasse negamus, fallimur, et nulla est in nobis veritas;   40
If we say that we have no sin, we deceive ourselves, and there's
   no truth in us. Why, then, belike we must sin, and so conse-
   quently die:
Ay, we must die an everlasting death.

What doctrine call you this: *Che sera, sera,*
What will be, shall be? Divinity, adieu!
These metaphysics of magicians
And necromantic books are heavenly;
Lines, circles, scenes, letters, and characters;
Ay, these are those that Faustus most desires.   50
O, what a world of profit and delight,
Of power, of honour, of omnipotence,
Is promis'd to the studious artisan!
All things that move between the quiet poles
Shall be at my command: emperors and kings
Are but obeyed in their several provinces,
Nor can they raise the wind, or rend the clouds;
But his dominion that exceeds in this,
Stretcheth as far as doth the mind of man;
A sound magician is a mighty god: 60
Here, Faustus, tire thy brains to gain a deity.

Enter WAGNER

Wagner, commend me to my dearest friends,
The German Valdes and Cornelius;
Request them earnestly to visit me.
WAGNER. I will, sir.   [*Exit.*
FAUSTUS. Their conference will be a greater help to me
Than all my labours, plod I ne'er so fast.

Enter GOOD ANGEL *and* EVIL ANGEL

G. ANGEL. O, Faustus, lay that damned book aside,
And gaze not on it, lest it tempt thy soul,
And heap God's heavy wrath upon thy head!   70
Read, read the Scriptures:—that is blasphemy.
E. ANGEL. Go forward, Faustus, in that famous art
Wherein all Nature's treasure is contain'd:
Be thou on earth as Jove is in the sky,
Lord and commander of these elements.   [*Exeunt* ANGELS.

FAUSTUS. How am I glutted with conceit of this!
    Shall I make spirits fetch me what I please,
    Resolve me of all ambiguities,
    Perform what desperate enterprise I will?
    I'll have them fly to India for gold,   80
    Ransack the ocean for orient pearl,
    And search all corners of the new-found world
    For pleasant fruits and princely delicates;
    I'll have them read me strange philosophy,
    And tell the secrets of all foreign kings;
    I'll have them wall all Germany with brass,
    And make swift Rhine circle fair Wertenberg;
    I'll have them fill the public schools with silk,
    Wherewith the students shall be bravely clad;
    I'll levy soldiers with the coin they bring,   90
    And chase the Prince of Parma from our land,
    And reign sole king of all the provinces;
    Yea, stranger engines for the brunt of war,
    Than was the fiery keel at Antwerp's bridge,
    I'll make my servile spirits to invent.

      [*Instructed by* VALDES *and* CORNELIUS, FAUSTUS *learns how
    to call upon the spirits of darkness. Through the agency of*
    MEPHISTOPHILIS, *he enters into a contract with* LUCIFER,
    who promises, in return for FAUSTUS' *soul, to grant him
    everything that he desires during a period of twenty-four years.*
    FAUSTUS' *use of his power is for the most part trivial, in
    contrast with the magnificent suggestions of his first imagin-
    ings. The twenty-four years draw to their close with but little
    accomplished.*]

SCENE II

FAUSTUS *and* MEPHISTOPHILIS

Enter an OLD MAN

OLD MAN. Ah, Doctor Faustus, that I might prevail
    To guide thy steps unto the way of life,
    By which sweet path thou mayst attain the goal

That shall conduct thee to celestial rest!
Break heart, drop blood, and mingle it with tears,
Tears falling from repentant heaviness
Of thy most vile and loathsome filthiness,
The stench whereof corrupts the inward soul
With such flagitious crimes of heinous sin
As no commiseration may expel,   10
But mercy, Faustus, of thy Saviour sweet,
Whose blood alone must wash away thy guilt.

FAUSTUS. Where art thou, Faustus? Wretch, what hast thou done?
Damn'd art thou, Faustus, damn'd; despair and die!
Hell calls for right, and with a roaring voice
Says, 'Faustus, come; thine hour is almost come;'
And Faustus now will come to do thee right.

[MEPHISTOPHILIS *gives him a dagger.*

OLD MAN. Ah, stay, good Faustus, stay thy desperate steps!
I see an angel hovers o'er thy head,
And, with a vial full of precious grace,   20
Offers to pour the same into thy soul:
Then call for mercy, and avoid despair.

FAUSTUS. Ah, my sweet friend, I feel
Thy words to comfort my distressed soul!
Leave me a while to ponder on my sins.

OLD MAN. I go, sweet Faustus; but with heavy cheer,
Fearing the ruin of thy hopeless soul.   [*Exit.*

FAUSTUS. Accursed Faustus, where is mercy now?
I do repent; and yet I do despair:
Hell strives with grace for conquest in my breast: 30
What shall I do to shun the snares of death?

MEPH. Thou traitor, Faustus; I arrest thy soul
For disobedience to my sovereign lord:
Revolt, or I'll in piece-meal tear thy flesh.

FAUSTUS. Sweet Mephistophilis, entreat thy lord
To pardon my unjust presumption,
And with my blood again I will confirm
My former vow I made to Lucifer.

MEPH. Do it, then, quickly, with unfeigned heart,
   Lest greater danger do attend thy drift.   40
FAUSTUS. Torment, sweet friend, that base and crooked age,
   That durst dissuade me from thy Lucifer,
   With greatest torments that our hell affords.
MEPH. His faith is great; I cannot touch his soul;
   But what I may afflict his body with
   I will attempt, which is but little worth.
FAUSTUS. One thing, good servant, let me crave of thee,
   To glut the longing of my heart's desire,—
   That I might have unto my paramour
   That heavenly Helen which I saw of late,   50
   Whose sweet embracings may extinguish clean
   Those thoughts that do dissuade me from my vow,
   And keep mine oath I made to Lucifer.
MEPH. Faustus, this, or what else thou shalt desire,
   Shall be perform'd in twinkling of an eye.

Enter HELEN

FAUSTUS. Was this the face that launch'd a thousand ships,
   And burnt the topless towers of Ilium?
   Sweet Helen, make me immortal with a kiss.—

                           [*Kisses her.*

   Her lips suck forth my soul: see, where it flies!—
   Come, Helen, come, give me my soul again.   60
   Here will I dwell, for heaven is in these lips,
   And all is dross that is not Helena.
   I will be Paris, and for love of thee,
   Instead of Troy, shall Wertenberg be sack'd;
   And I will combat with weak Menelaus,
   And wear thy colours on my plumed crest;
   Yes, I will wound Achilles in the heel,
   And then return to Helen for a kiss.
   O, thou art fairer than the evening air
   Clad in the beauty of a thousand stars;   70
   Brighter art thou than flaming Jupiter

When he appear'd to hapless Semele;
More lovely than the monarch of the sky
In wanton Arethusa's azur'd arms;
And none but thou shalt be my paramour!   [*Exeunt.*

Enter the OLD MAN

OLD MAN. Accursed Faustus, miserable man,
That from thy soul exclud'st the grace of heaven,
And fly'st the throne of his tribunal-seat!

Enter DEVILS

Satan begins to sift me with his pride:
As in this furnace God shall try my faith,   80
My faith, vile hell, shall triumph over thee,
Ambitious fiends, see how the heavens smile
At your repulse, and laugh your state to scorn!
Hence, hell! for hence I fly unto my God.
      [*Exeunt—on one side,* DEVILS; *on the other,* OLD MAN.

SCENE III

Enter FAUSTUS, *with* SCHOLARS

FAUSTUS. Ah gentlemen!

FIRST SCHOL. What ails Faustus?

FAUSTUS. Ah my sweet chamber-fellow! had I lived with thee,
then had I lived still, but now I die eternally. Look, comes he
not? Comes he not?

SEC. SCHOL. What means Faustus?

THIRD SCHOL. Belike he is grown into some sickness by being
over-solitary.

FIRST SCHOL. If it be so, we'll have physicians to cure him.—
'Tis but a surfeit; never fear, man.   10

FAUSTUS. A surfeit of deadly sin, that hath damned both body and
soul.

SEC. SCHOL. Yet, Faustus, look up to heaven; remember God's
mercies are infinite.

FAUSTUS. But Faustus' offence can ne'er be pardoned. The serpent that tempted Eve may be saved, but not Faustus. Ah, gentlemen, hear me with patience, and tremble not at my speeches! Though my heart pants and quivers to remember that I have been a student here these thirty years, O, would I had never seen Wertenberg, never read book! and what wonders I have done, all Germany can witness, yea, all the world; for which Faustus hath lost both Germany and the world, yea, heaven itself, heaven, the seat of God, the throne of the blessed, the kingdom of joy; and must remain in hell for ever, hell, ah, hell, for ever! Sweet friends, what shall become of Faustus, being in hell for ever?   26

THIRD SCHOL. Yet, Faustus, call on God.

FAUSTUS. On God, whom Faustus hath abjured! on God, whom Faustus hath blasphemed! Ah, my God, I would weep! but the devil draws in my tears. Gush forth blood, instead of tears! yea, life and soul! O, he stays my tongue! I would lift up my hands; but see, they hold them, they hold them!   32

ALL. Who, Faustus?

FAUSTUS. Lucifer and Mephistophilis. Ah, gentlemen, I gave them my soul for my cunning!

ALL. God forbid!

FAUSTUS. God forbade it, indeed; but Faustus hath done it: for vain pleasure of twenty-four years hath Faustus lost eternal joy and felicity. I writ a bill with mine own blood: the date is expired; the time will come, and he will fetch me.   40

FIRST SCHOL. Why did not Faustus tell us of this before, that divines might have prayed for thee?

FAUSTUS. Oft have I thought to have done so; but the devil threatened to tear me in pieces, if I named God; to fetch both body and soul, if I once gave ear to divinity: and now 'tis too late. Gentlemen, away, lest you perish with me.

SEC. SCHOL. O, what shall we do to save Faustus?

FAUSTUS. Talk not of me, but save yourselves, and depart.

THIRD SCHOL. God will strengthen me; I will stay with Faustus.

FIRST SCHOL. Tempt not God, sweet friend; but let us into the next room, and there pray for him.   51

FAUSTUS. Ay, pray for me, pray for me; and what noise soever ye
  hear, come not unto me, for nothing can rescue me.

SEC. SCHOL. Pray thou, and we will pray that God may have
  mercy upon thee.

FAUSTUS. Gentlemen, farewell: if I live till morning, I'll visit
  you; if not, Faustus is gone to hell.

ALL. Faustus, farewell.

> [*Exeunt* SCHOLARS.—*The clock strikes eleven.*

FAUSTUS. Ah, Faustus,

  Now hast thou but one bare hour to live,   60
  And then thou must be damn'd perpetually!
  Stand still, you ever-moving spheres of heaven,
  That time may cease, and midnight never come;
  Fair Nature's eye, rise, rise again, and make
  Perpetual day; or let this hour be but
  A year, a month, a week, a natural day,
  That Faustus may repent and save his soul!
  O lente, lente currite, noctis equi!
  The stars move still, time runs, the clock will strike,
  The devil will come, and Faustus must be damn'd.   70
  O, I'll leap up to my God!—Who pulls me down?—
  See, see, where Christ's blood streams in the firmament!
  One drop would save my soul, half a drop: ah, my Christ!—
  Ah, rend not my heart for naming of my Christ!
  Yet will I call on him: O, spare me, Lucifer!—
  Where is it now? 'tis gone: and see, where God
  Stretcheth out his arm, and bends his ireful brows!
  Mountains and hills, come, come, and fall on me,
  And hide me from the heavy wrath of God!
  No, no!   80
  Then will I headlong run into the earth:
  Earth, gape! O, no, it will not harbour me!
  You stars that reign'd at my nativity,
  Whose influence hath allotted death and hell,
  Now draw up Faustus, like a foggy mist,
  Into the entrails of yon labouring cloud,

That, when you vomit forth into the air,
My limbs may issue from your smoky mouths,
So that my soul may but ascend to heaven!

       [The clock strikes the half-hour.

Ah, half the hour is past! 'twill all be past anon. 90
O God,
If thou wilt not have mercy on my soul,
Yet for Christ's sake, whose blood hath ransom'd me,
Impose some end to my incessant pain;
Let Faustus live in hell a thousand years,
A hundred thousand, and at last be sav'd.
O, no end is limited to damned souls!
Why wert thou not a creature wanting soul?
Or why is this immortal that thou hast?
Ah, Pythagoras' metempsychosis, were that true, 100
This soul should fly from me, and I be chang'd
Unto some brutish beast! All beasts are happy,
For, when they die,
Their souls are soon dissolv'd in elements;
But mine must live still to be plagu'd in hell.
Curs'd be the parents that engender'd me!
No, Faustus, curse thyself, curse Lucifer,
That hath depriv'd thee of the joys of heaven!

        [The clock strikes twelve.

O, it strikes, it strikes! Now body, turn to air,
Or Lucifer will bear thee quick to hell! 110
O soul, be chang'd into little water-drops,
And fall into the ocean, ne'er be found!

Enter DEVILS

My God, my God, look not so fierce on me!
Adders and serpents, let me breathe a while!
Ugly hell, gape not! come not, Lucifer!
I'll burn my books!—Ah, Mephistophilis!

      [Exeunt DEVILS *with* FAUSTUS.

E

Enter CHORUS

CHORUS. Cut is the branch that might have grown full straight,
    And burned is Apollo's laurel-bough
    That sometime grew within this learned man.
    Faustus is gone: regard his hellish fall,   120
    Whose fiendful fortune may exhort the wise,
    Only to wonder at unlawful things,
    Whose deepness doth entice such forward wits
    To practise more than heavenly power permits.   [*Exit.*

POINTS FOR DISCUSSION

1. Why is the hero of a tragedy so often a king?
2. Faustus is only a German doctor. In what, then, does his greatness consist?
3. Which passage in the play links it with the Morality Plays? Find another passage which is a similar but less obvious link.
4. What means does Marlowe use to win our sympathy for Faustus in his ambition for limitless power?
5. The greater part of the play is taken up with the 'inner conflict', the conflict in the mind of Faustus. Is there any 'external conflict'?
6. How does the last speech of Faustus illustrate the difference between 'dramatic time' and real time? Would the speech be improved if they were made to coincide?
7. Marlowe 'concentrated attention upon the greatness of the man, rather than upon the greatness of his overthrow'. Illustrate this from the extract.

MACBETH

By WILLIAM SHAKESPEARE

THE STORY. At the beginning of the play Macbeth appears as the deliverer of his country from foreign invasion, winning

Golden opinions from all sorts of people

and regarded by his king with absolute confidence. Line after line of his speeches shows how vividly aware he is of the significance of human actions and of the irrevocable consequences of crime; and yet he himself murders Duncan, the king, whose virtues he freely acknowledges. Such a deed seems inexplicably unnatural,

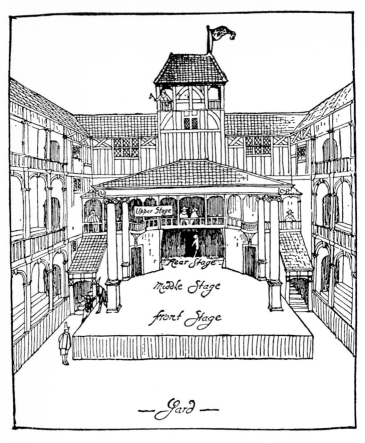

THE FORTUNE THEATRE
(An Elizabethan setting)

'DESIGN FOR *MACBETH*', VICTOR HEMBROW

(A modern setting)

and the strange horror of the situation is partly expressed by the
association of the crime with the prophecies of the Three Witches,
who first appear to Macbeth as he is returning from the battle
against the invading armies. They give utterance to his secret
ambition by foretelling that he will become king. He goes through
a time of inner conflict, and finally allows his own ambition and
the taunting insistence of his wife to drive him to the murder. After
Duncan has been killed, Macbeth's imagination lights up the future.
He knows that restfulness has gone from him for ever, that

> Glamis hath murder'd sleep, and therefore Cawdor
> Shall sleep no more,—Macbeth shall sleep no more!

and yet all this intensity of imagination does not hold him back
from deeds of even greater foulness than that which he has already
committed. With growing callousness he murders Banquo, Lady
Macduff and her son, and multiplies his crimes until Ross says of
Scotland:

> It cannot
> Be called our mother, but our grave: where nothing,
> But who knows nothing, is once seen to smile;
> Where sighs, and groans, and shrieks that rent the air,
> Are made, not markt; where violent sorrow seems
> A modern ecstasy; the dead man's knell
> Is there scarce askt for who; and good men's lives
> Expire before the flowers in their caps,
> Dying or e'er they sicken.

At the end of the play he is a sorry figure, with only flashes of
his former greatness to keep the audience mindful of the magnitude
of his disaster, and to emphasize the contrast between the imagina-
tive power of the man and the worthlessness of the life which he
has lived. The extract is taken from Act II, which is concerned
with the murder of Duncan.

SCENE I

Inverness. Court of MACBETH'S *castle*

Enter BANQUO, *and* FLEANCE *with a torch before him*

BANQUO. How goes the night, boy?

FLEANCE. The moon is down; I have not heard the clock.

BANQUO. And she goes down at twelve.

FLEANCE. I take 't, 'tis later, sir.

BANQUO. Hold, take my sword:—there's husbandry in heaven,
Their candles are all out:—take thee that too.—
A heavy summons lies like lead upon me,
And yet I would not sleep:—merciful powers,
Restrain in me the cursed thoughts that nature
Gives way to in repose!—Give me my sword.—   10
Who's there?

Enter MACBETH, *and a* SERVANT *with a torch*

MACBETH. A friend.

BANQUO. What, sir, not yet at rest? The king's a-bed:
He hath been in unusual pleasure, and
Sent forth great largess to your officers:
This diamond he greets your wife withal,
By the name of most kind hostess; and shut up
In measureless content.

MACBETH.   Being unprepared,
Our will became the servant to defect;
Which else should free have wrought.

BANQUO.   All's well.—   20
I dreamt last night of the three weird sisters:
To you they have show'd some truth.

MACBETH.   I think not of them:
Yet, when we can entreat an hour to serve,
We would spend it in some words upon that business,
If you would grant the time.

BANQUO.   At your kind'st leisure.

MACBETH. If you shall cleave to my consent,—when 'tis,
It shall make honour for you.

BANQUO.   So I lose none
In seeking to augment it, but still keep
My bosom franchised, and allegiance clear,
I shall be counsell'd.

MACBETH.   Good repose the while!   30

BANQUO. Thanks, sir; the like to you!

                              [*Exeunt* BANQUO *and* FLEANCE.

MACBETH. Go bid thy mistress, when my drink is ready,
She strike upon the bell. Get thee to bed.

[Exit SERVANT.

Is this a dagger which I see before me,
The handle toward my hand? Come, let me clutch thee:—
I have thee not, and yet I see thee still.
Art thou not, fatal vision, sensible
To feeling as to sight? or art thou but
A dagger of the mind, a false creation,
Proceeding from the heat-oppressed brain? 40
I see thee yet, in form as palpable
As this which now I draw.
Thou marshall'st me the way that I was going;
And such an instrument I was to use.
Mine eyes are made the fools o' th' other senses,
Or else worth all the rest: I see thee still;
And on thy blade and dudgeon gouts of blood,
Which was not so before.—There's no such thing:
It is the bloody business which informs
Thus to mine eyes.—Now o'er the one half-world 50
Nature seems dead, and wicked dreams abuse
The curtain'd sleep; now witchcraft celebrates
Pale Hecate's offerings; and wither'd murder,
Alarum'd by his sentinel, the wolf,
Whose howl's his watch, thus with his stealthy pace,
With Tarquin's ravishing strides, towards his design
Moves like a ghost.—Thou sure and firm-set earth,
Hear not my steps, which way they walk, for fear
Thy very stones prate of my whereabout,
And take the present horror from the time, 60
Which now suits with it.—Whiles I threat, he lives:
Words to the heat of deeds too cold breath gives.

[A bell rings.

I go, and it is done; the bell invites me.
Hear it not, Duncan; for it is a knell
That summons thee to heaven or to hell. *[Exit.*

SCENE II

The same

Enter LADY MACBETH

LADY MACBETH. That which hath made them drunk hath made
    me bold;
  What hath quencht them hath given me fire.—
         Hark!—Peace!
  It was the owl that shriekt, the fatal bellman,
  Which gives the stern'st good-night.—He is about it:
  The doors are open; and the surfeited grooms
  Do mock their charge with snores: I have drugg'd their possets,
  That death and nature do contend about them,
  Whether they live or die.
MACBETH [*within*].   Who's there? what, ho!
LADY MACBETH. Alack, I am afraid they have awaked,   10
  And 'tis not done:—th' attempt, and not the deed,
  Confounds us.—Hark!—I laid their daggers ready;
  He could not miss 'em.—Had he not resembled
  My father as he slept, I had done 't.—My husband!

Enter MACBETH

MACBETH. I have done the deed.—Didst thou not hear a noise?
LADY MACBETH. I heard the owl scream and the crickets cry.
  Did not you speak?
MACBETH.   When?
LADY MACBETH.   Now.
MACBETH.   As I descended?
LADY MACBETH. Ay.
MACBETH. Hark!—
  Who lies i' th' second chamber?
LADY MACBETH.   Donalbain.   20
MACBETH. This is a sorry sight.   [*Looking on his hands.*
LADY MACBETH. A foolish thought, to say a sorry sight.
MACBETH. There's one did laugh in 's sleep, and one cried 'Mur-
  der!'

That they did wake each other: I stood and heard them:
But they did say their prayers, and addrest them
Again to sleep.

LADY MACBETH.   There are two lodged together.

MACBETH.   One cried 'God bless us!' and 'Amen!' the other;
As they had seen me with these hangman's hands.
Listening their fear, I could not say 'Amen!'
When they did say 'God bless us!'

LADY MACBETH.   Consider it not so deeply. 30

MACBETH.   But wherefore could not I pronounce 'Amen'?
I had most need of blessing, and 'Amen'
Stuck in my throat.

LADY MACBETH.   These deeds must not be thought
After these ways; so, it will make us mad.

MACBETH.   Methought I heard a voice cry 'Sleep no more!
Macbeth does murder sleep,'—the innocent sleep,
Sleep that knits up the ravell'd sleave of care,
The death of each day's life, sore labour's bath,
Balm of hurt minds, great nature's second course,
Chief nourisher in life's feast,—

LADY MACBETH.   What do you mean?   40

MACBETH.   Still it cried 'Sleep no more!' to all the house:
'Glamis hath murder'd sleep, and therefore Cawdor
Shall sleep no more,—Macbeth shall sleep no more!'

LADY MACBETH.   Who was it that thus cried? Why, worthy thane,
You do unbend your noble strength, to think
So brainsickly of things.—Go get some water,
And wash this filthy witness from your hand.—
Why did you bring these daggers from the place?
They must lie there: go carry them, and smear
The sleepy grooms with blood.

MACBETH.   I'll go no more: 50
I am afraid to think what I have done;
Look on 't again I dare not.

LADY MACBETH.   Infirm of purpose!
Give me the daggers: the sleeping and the dead

Are but as pictures: 'tis the eye of childhood
That fears a painted devil. If he do bleed,
I'll gild the faces of the grooms withal;
For it must seem their guilt.   [*Exit. Knock within.*
MACBETH.   Whence is that knocking?
How is't with me, when every noise appals me?
What hands are here? ha! they pluck out mine eyes!
Will all great Neptune's ocean wash this blood   60
Clean from my hand? No; this my hand will rather
The multitudinous seas incarnadine,
Making the green one red.

Enter LADY MACBETH

LADY MACBETH. My hands are of your colour; but I shame
To wear a heart so white. [*Knock.*] I hear a knocking
At the south entry:—retire we to our chamber:
A little water clears us of this deed:
How easy is it, then! Your constancy
Hath left you unattended.—[*Knock.*] Hark! more knocking:
Get on your nightgown, lest occasion call us,   70
And show us to be watchers:—be not lost
So poorly in your thoughts.
MACBETH. To know my deed, 'twere best not know myself.
                                        [*Knock.*
Wake Duncan with thy knocking! I would thou couldst!
                                        [*Exeunt.*

POINTS FOR DISCUSSION

1. The description of the scenery at the beginning of the extract has
   been added by modern editors. With what part of the scenery is
   Shakespeare concerned? What other scenery is described later, and
   for what purpose?

2. What are the two topics of conversation between Macbeth and Banquo
   in Scene I? What dramatic purpose is served by the introduction of
   these two topics?

3. What is the climax of Scene I?

4. What insight does Macbeth's vision of the dagger give us into his character?

5. Which two passages towards the beginning of Scene II suggest that Lady Macbeth is less bold than her husband? When does she appear bolder than he?

6. The murder of Duncan, like the suicide of Jocasta and the blinding of Oedipus, is committed 'off stage'. How do the methods of presentation used by Shakespeare differ from those of Sophocles?

7. After the murder of Duncan, Macbeth has an almost unbearable sense of ..., which is absent in his wife. Supply the word which has been omitted, and prove that you are right in your choice by quotations from the play.

8. Which of Macbeth's speeches in these two scenes support the statement that he is a poet, as well as a general?

9. What part is played by noise in these two scenes?

10. Consider the merits of Victor Hembrow's 'Design for *Macbeth*'. Do you approve of this kind of setting for a Shakespearean play?

CHAPTER IV

TWO KINDS OF COMEDY

THE COMEDY OF HUMOURS

THERE was another kind of Elizabethan play, revived from earlier examples by Shakespeare's friend and rival, Ben Jonson. He developed a kind of comedy which was popular for some years.

Most children, at some time in their lives, are amused by a jack-in-the-box: they press the button, and out he comes. Their cry of joy seems to be made up of a mixture of expectation and surprise; they know that the little black face will pop up when they press the button, but even so the face is surprising when it suddenly jerks up before them. In much the same way people enjoyed watching the comedies of Ben Jonson. The characters were like so many jack-in-the-boxes, they always did the same kind of thing.[1] If a man was jealous, then he remained jealous throughout the play, and as soon as any one came within sight of his wife the audience knew that he was going to be worried. The characters were types rather than people, with names like George Downright (a plain squire), or Brainworm (a clever schemer), to act as labels by which the audience could recognize them. This method of comedy was linked with a medical theory of the time, which said that a man's temperament was determined by the proportion of four fluids or 'humours' in his body. There was the sanguine humour, the choleric, the phlegmatic, and the melancholic. Too much of any one of them made a man eccentric or 'humorous'; in the words of Ben Jonson himself:

. . . in every human body
The choler, melancholy, phlegm, and blood,

[1] See *Shakespeare Studies*, E. E. Stoll (Macmillan, 1927).

By reason that they flow continually
In some one part, and are not continent,
Receive the name of humours. Now thus far
It may, by metaphor, apply itself
Unto the general disposition:
As when some one peculiar quality
Doth so possess a man, that it doth draw
All his affects, his spirits, and his powers,
In their confluxions, all to run one way,
This may be truly said to be a humour.

This method of comedy, in a slightly developed form, reached its highest perfection in France in the plays of Molière, who used it with exquisite effect. In England it did not prove popular for long. English audiences seem to be warmer-hearted than the French; they like to sympathize with the characters on the stage, and laugh with them as well as at them. To enjoy a comedy of 'humour' written in the manner of Ben Jonson, the audience have to detach themselves from sympathy with the people in the play. Sorrow for a man who is jealous makes him cease to be funny. Englishmen preferred a character like Falstaff, who enjoyed his own absurdities and laughed along with the audience.

Of this kind of comedy, one of the most famous is *Every Man in His Humour*, by Ben Jonson. The title summarizes the play. Most of the characters have some foible or eccentricity, and it is the interplay of these 'humours' which makes the comedy. Knowell is an elderly gentleman who is excessively afraid that his son, Edward Knowell, will waste his time with idle gallants about the city, instead of making progress with his studies. His fears seem to be realized when he intercepts a letter for his son from Wellbred, asking him to join a party at the 'Windmill'. He follows his son, determined to expose his folly, but he is prevented from doing this by the tricks and plots of his own servant Brainworm, who is determined to win the favour of his future master, young Knowell. In the end, Brainworm becomes entangled in his own plots; but he has given Edward Knowell opportunity to pay his addresses to Bridget, Wellbred's sister, and all ends happily, as Old Knowell approves of the match.

Among the party of gallants with whom Wellbred is amusing himself at the 'Windmill' is a Captain Bobadill, a great boaster, and his admirer, Mathew, 'a country gull'. Downright, Wellbred's half-brother, is much opposed to the company he keeps, and is particularly enraged at Bobadill, who has affected to despise him. The extracts chosen are concerned with this Captain Bobadill, who has become one of the most famous characters of the play.

EVERY MAN IN HIS HUMOUR

By BEN JONSON

SCENE I. *A Room in* COB'S *House.* BOBADILL *discovered lying on a bench*

BOB. Hostess, hostess!

Enter TIB

TIB. What say you, sir?

BOB. A cup of thy small beer, sweet hostess.

TIB. Sir, there's a gentleman below would speak with you.

BOB. A gentleman! 'odso, I am not within.

TIB. My husband told him you were, sir.

BOB. What a plague—what meant he?

MAT. [*below.*] Captain Bobadill!

BOB. Who's there!—Take away the bason, good hostess;—Come up, sir.

TIB. He would desire you to come up, sir. You come into a cleanly house, here!

Enter MATHEW

MAT. Save you, sir; save you, captain!

BOB. Gentle master Mathew! Is it you, sir? Please you to sit down.

MAT. Thank you, good captain; you may see I am somewhat audacious.

BOB. Not so, sir. I was requested to supper last night by a sort of gallants, where you were wished for, and drunk to, I assure you.

MAT. Vouchsafe me, by whom, good captain?

BOB. Marry, by young Wellbred, and others.—Why, hostess, a stool here for this gentleman.

MAT. No haste, sir, 'tis very well.

BOB. Body o' me! it was so late ere we parted last night, I can scarce open my eyes yet; I was but new risen, as you came; how passes the day abroad, sir? you can tell.

MAT. Faith, some half hour to seven; Now, trust me, you have an exceeding fine lodging here, very neat, and private.

BOB. Ay, sir: sit down, I pray you. Master Mathew, in any case possess no gentlemen of our acquaintance with notice of my lodging.

MAT. Who? I, sir? no.

BOB. Not that I need to care who know it, for the cabin is convenient; but in regard I would not be too popular, and generally visited, as some are.

MAT. True, captain, I conceive you.

BOB. So, so; it's the fashion gentlemen now use.

MAT. Troth, captain, and now you speak of the fashion, master Wellbred's elder brother and I are fallen out exceedingly: this other day, I happened to enter into some discourse of a hanger, which, I assure you, both for fashion and workmanship, was most peremptory beautiful and gentlemanlike: yet he condemned, and cried it down for the most pied and ridiculous that ever he saw.

BOB. Squire Downright, the half-brother, was't not?

MAT. Ay, sir, he.

BOB. Hang him, rook! he! why he has no more judgment than a malt-horse: by St. George, I wonder you'd lose a thought upon such an animal; the most peremptory absurd clown of Christendom, this day, he is holden. I protest to you, as I am a gentleman and a soldier, I ne'er changed with his like. By his discourse, he should eat nothing but hay; he was born for the manger, pannier, or pack-saddle. He has not so much as a good phrase in his belly, but all old iron and rusty proverbs: a good commodity for some smith to make hob-nails of.

MAT. Ay, and he thinks to carry it away with his manhood still, where he comes: he brags he will give me the bastinado, as I hear.

BOB. How! he the bastinado! how came he by that word, trow?

MAT. Nay, indeed, he said cudgel me; I termed it so, for my more grace.

BOB. That may be: for I was sure it was none of his word; but when, when said he so?

MAT. Faith, yesterday, they say; a young gallant, a friend of mine, told me so.

BOB. By the foot of Pharaoh, an 'twere my case now, I should send him a chartel presently. The bastinado! a most proper and sufficient dependence, warranted by the great Caranza. Come hither, you shall chartel him; I'll shew you a trick or two you shall kill him with at pleasure; the first stoccata, if you will, by this air.

MAT. Indeed, you have absolute knowledge in the mystery, I have heard, sir.

BOB. Of whom, of whom, have you heard it, I beseech you?

MAT. Troth, I have heard it spoken of divers, that you have very rare, and un-in-one-breath-utterable skill, sir.

BOB. By heaven, no, not I; no skill in the earth; some small rudiments in the science, as to know my time, distance, or so. I have professed it more for noblemen and gentlemen's use, than mine own practice, I assure you.—Hostess, accommodate us with another bed-staff here quickly. Lend us another bed-

staff—the woman does not understand the words of action.—
Look you, sir: exalt not your point above this state, at any
hand, and let your poniard maintain your defence, thus:—
give it the gentleman, and leave us. [*Exit* TIB.] So, sir. Come
on: O, twine your body more about, that you may fall to
a more sweet, comely, gentlemanlike guard; so! indifferent:
hollow your body more, sir, thus: now, stand fast o' your left
leg, note your distance, keep your due proportion of time—
oh, you disorder your point most irregularly.

MAT. How is the bearing of it now, sir?

BOB. O, out of measure ill: a well-experienced hand would pass
upon you at pleasure.

MAT. How mean you, sir, pass upon me?

BOB. Why, thus, sir,—make a thrust at me—[MASTER MATHEW
pushes at BOBADILL] come in upon the answer, control your
point, and make a full career at the body: the best-practised
gallants of the time name it the passado; a most desperate
thrust, believe it.

MAT. Well, come, sir.

BOB. Why, you do not manage your weapon with any facility or
grace to invite me. I have no spirit to play with you; your
dearth of judgment renders you tedious.

MAT. But one venue, sir.

BOB. Venue! fie; the most gross denomination as ever I heard:
O, the stoccata, while you live, sir; note that.—Come, put on
your cloak, and we'll go to some private place where you are
acquainted; some tavern, or so—and have a bit. I'll send for
one of these fencers, and he shall breathe you, by my direction;
and then I will teach you your trick: you shall kill him with it
at the first, if you please. Why, I will learn you, by the true
judgment of the eye, hand, and foot, to control any enemy's
point in the world. Should your adversary confront you with
a pistol, 'twere nothing, by this hand! you should, by the same
rule, control his bullet, in a line, except it were hail shot, and
spread. What money have you about you, master Mathew?

MAT. Faith, I have not past a two shilling or so.

BOB. 'Tis somewhat with the least; but come; we will have a
bunch of radish and salt to taste our wine, and a pipe of tobacco
to close the orifice of the stomach: and then we'll call upon
young Wellbred: perhaps we shall meet the Corydon his
brother there, and put him to the question.

SCENE II. *The Old Jewry. A Room in the Windmill Tavern*

Enter MASTER MATHEW, WELLBRED, *and* BOBADILL

MAT. Yes, faith, sir, we were at your lodging to seek you too.

WEL. Oh, I came not there to-night.

BOB. Your brother delivered us as much.

WEL. Who, my brother Downright?

BOB. He. Mr. Wellbred, I know not in what kind you hold me;
but let me say to you this: as sure as honour, I esteem it so
much out of the sunshine of reputation, to throw the least
beam of regard upon such a—

WEL. Sir, I must hear no ill words of my brother.

BOB. I protest to you, as I have a thing to be saved about me,
I never saw any gentlemanlike part—

WEL. Good captain, faces about to some other discourse.

BOB. With your leave, sir, an there were no more men living
upon the face of the earth, I should not fancy him, by St.
George!

MAT. Troth, nor I; he is of a rustical cut, I know not how: he
doth not carry himself like a gentleman of fashion.

WEL. Oh, master Mathew, that's a grace peculiar but to a few,
quos aequus amavit Jupiter.

MAT. I understand you, sir.

WEL. No question, you do,—or do you not, sir.

Enter EDWARD KNOWELL *and* MASTER STEPHEN

Ned Knowell! by my soul, welcome: how dost thou, sweet
spirit, my genius? 'Slid, I shall love Apollo and the mad
Thespian girls the better, while I live, for this, my dear Fury;
now, I see there's some love in thee. Sirrah, these be the two

I writ to thee of: nay, what a drowsy humour is this now! why dost thou not speak?

E. KNOW. Oh, you are a fine gallant; you sent me a rare letter.

WEL. Why, was't not rare?

E. KNOW. Yes, I'll be sworn, I was ne'er guilty of reading the like; match it in all Pliny, or Symmachus's epistles, and I'll have my judgment burn'd in the ear for a rogue: make much of thy vein, for it is inimitable. But I marvel what camel it was, that had the carriage of it; for, doubtless, he was no ordinary beast that brought it.

WEL. Why?

E. KNOW. Why, say'st thou! why, dost thou think that any reasonable creature, especially in the morning, the sober time of the day too, could have mistaken my father for me?

WEL. 'Slid, you jest, I hope.

E. KNOW. Indeed, the best use we can turn it to, is to make a jest on't, now: but I'll assure you, my father had the full view of your flourishing style some hour before I saw it.

WEL. What a dull slave was this! but, sirrah, what said he to it, i'faith?

E. KNOW. Nay, I know not what he said; but I have a shrewd guess what he thought.

WEL. What, what?

E. KNOW. Marry, that thou art some strange, dissolute young fellow, and I—a grain or two better, for keeping thee company.

WEL. Tut! that thought is like the moon in her last quarter, 'twill change shortly: but, sirrah, I pray thee be acquainted with my two hang-by's here; thou wilt take exceeding pleasure in them if thou hear'st 'em once go; my wind-instruments; I'll wind them up—But what strange piece of silence is this, the sign of the Dumb Man?

E. KNOW. Oh, sir, a kinsman of mine, one that may make your music the fuller, an he please; he has his humour, sir.

WEL. Oh, what is't, what is't?

E. KNOW. Nay, I'll neither do your judgment nor his folly that

F

wrong, as to prepare your apprehension: I'll leave him to the mercy of your search; if you can take him, so!

WEL. Well, captain Bobadill, master Mathew, pray you know this gentleman here; he is a friend of mine, and one that will deserve your affection. I know not your name, sir, [*to* STEPHEN] but I shall be glad of any occasion to render me more familiar to you.

STEP. My name is master Stephen, sir; I am this gentleman's own cousin, sir; his father is mine uncle, sir; I am somewhat melancholy, but you shall command me, sir, in whatsoever is incident to a gentleman.

BOB. Sir, I must tell you this, I am no general man; but for master Wellbred's sake, (you may embrace it at what height of favour you please), I do communicate with you, and conceive you to be a gentleman of some parts; I love few words.

E. KNOW. And I fewer, sir; I have scarce enough to thank you.

MAT. But are you, indeed, sir, so given to it?

STEP. Ay, truly, sir, I am mightily given to melancholy.

MAT. Oh, it's your only fine humour, sir: your true melancholy breeds your perfect fine wit, sir. I am melancholy myself, divers times, sir, and then do I no more but take pen and paper, presently, and overflow you half a score, or a dozen of sonnets at a sitting.

E. KNOW. Sure he utters them then by the gross. [*Aside.*

STEP. Truly, sir, and I love such things out of measure.

E. KNOW. I'faith, better than in measure, I'll undertake.

MAT. Why, I pray you, sir, make use of my study, it's at your service.

STEP. I thank you, sir, I shall be bold, I warrant you; have you a stool there to be melancholy upon?

MAT. That I have, sir, and some papers there of mine own doing, at idle hours, that you'll say there's some sparks of wit in 'em, when you see them.

WEL. Would the sparks would kindle once, and become a fire amongst them! I might see self-love burnt for her heresy.

[*Aside.*

STEP. Cousin, is it well? am I melancholy enough?

E. KNOW. Oh ay, excellent.

WEL. Captain Bobadill, why muse you so?

E. KNOW. He is melancholy too.

BOB. Faith, sir, I was thinking of a most honourable piece of service, was performed tomorrow, being St. Mark's day, shall be
some ten years now.

E. KNOW. In what place, captain?

BOB. Why, at the beleaguering of Strigonium, where, in less than
two hours, seven hundred resolute gentlemen, as any were in
Europe, lost their lives upon the breach. I'll tell you, gentlemen, it was the first, but the best leaguer that ever I beheld
with these eyes, except the taking in of—what do you call it?
last year, by the Genoways; but that, of all other, was the most
fatal and dangerous exploit that ever I was ranged in, since I
first bore arms before the face of the enemy, as I am a gentleman
and a soldier!

STEP. So! I had as lief as an angel I could swear as well as that
gentleman.

E. KNOW. Then, you were a servitor at both, it seems; at Strigonium, and what do you call't?

BOB. O lord, sir! By St. George, I was the first man that entered
the breach; and had I not effected it with resolution, I had
been slain if I had had a million of lives.

E. KNOW. 'Twas pity you had not ten; a cat's and your own,
i'faith. But was it possible?

MAT. Pray you mark this discourse, sir.

STEP. So I do.

BOB. I assure you, upon my reputation, 'tis true, and yourself
shall confess.

E. KNOW. You must bring me to the rack, first.   [*Aside.*

BOB. Observe me judicially, sweet sir; they had planted me three
demi-culverins just in the mouth of the breach; now, sir, as
we were to give on, their master-gunner (a man of no mean
skill and mark, you must think,) confronts me with his linstock,
ready to give fire; I, spying his intendment, discharged my

petronel in his bosom, and with these single arms, my poor rapier, ran violently upon the Moors that guarded the ordnance, and put them pell-mell to the sword.

WEL. To the sword! To the rapier, captain.

E. KNOW. Oh, it was a good figure observed, sir: but did you all this, captain, without hurting your blade?

BOB. Without any impeach o' the earth: you shall perceive, sir. [*Shews his rapier.*] It is the most fortunate weapon that ever rid on poor gentleman's thigh. Shall I tell you, sir? You talk of Morglay, Excalibur, Durindana, or so; tut! I lend no credit to that is fabled of 'em: I know the virtue of mine own, and therefore I dare the boldlier maintain it.

STEP. I marvel whether it be a Toledo or no.

BOB. A most perfect Toledo, I assure you, sir.

STEP. I have a countryman of his here.

MAT. Pray you, let 's see, sir; yes, faith, it is.

BOB. This a Toledo! Pish!

STEP. Why do you pish, captain?

BOB. A Fleming, by heaven! I'll buy them for a guilder a-piece, an I would have a thousand of them.

E. KNOW. How say you, cousin? I told you thus much.

WEL. Where bought you it, master Stephen?

STEP. Of a scurvy rogue soldier: a hundred of lice go with him! He swore it was a Toledo.

BOB. A poor provant rapier, no better.

MAT. Mass, I think it be indeed, now I look on't better.

E. KNOW. Nay, the longer you look on't, the worse. Put it up, put it up.

STEP. Well, I will put it up; but by—I have forgot the captain's oath, I thought to have sworn by it—an e'er I meet him—

WEL. O, it is past help now, sir; you must have patience.

STEP. Whoreson, coney-hatching rascal! I could eat the very hilts for anger.

E. KNOW. A sign of good digestion; you have an ostrich stomach, cousin.

STEP. A stomach! would I had him here, you should see an I had a stomach.

WEL. It's better as it is.—Come, gentlemen, shall we go?

SCENE III. *Moorfields*

Enter MATHEW, E. KNOWELL, BOBADILL, *and* STEPHEN

MAT. Sir, did your eyes ever taste the like clown of him where we were to-day, Mr. Wellbred's half-brother? I think the whole earth cannot shew his parallel, by this daylight.

E. KNOW. We were now speaking of him: captain Bobadill tells me he is fallen foul of you too.

MAT. O, ay, sir, he threatened me with the bastinado.

BOB. Ay, but I think I taught you prevention this morning, for that: You shall kill him beyond question, if you be so generously minded.

MAT. Indeed, it is a most excellent trick.   [*Fences.*

BOB. O, you do not give spirit enough to your motion, you are too tardy, too heavy! O, it must be done like lightning, hay!
                    [*Practises at a post with his cudgel.*

MAT. Rare, captain!

BOB. Tut! 'tis nothing, an't be not done in a—punto.

E. KNOW. Captain, did you ever prove yourself upon any of our masters of defence, here?

MAT. O good sir! yes, I hope he has.

BOB. I will tell you, sir. Upon my first coming to the city, after my long travel for knowledge, in that mystery only, there came three or four of them to me, at a gentleman's house, where it was my chance to be resident at that time, to intreat my presence at their schools: and withal so much importuned me, that I protest to you, as I am a gentleman, I was ashamed of their rude demeanour out of all measure: Well, I told them that to come to a public school, they should pardon me, it was opposite, in diameter, to my humour; but if so be they would give their attendance at my lodging, I protested to do them what right or favour I could, as I was a gentleman, and so forth.

E. KNOW. So, sir! then you tried their skill?

BOB. Alas, soon tried: you shall hear, sir. Within two or three days after, they came; and, by honesty, fair sir, believe me, I graced them exceedingly, shewed them some two or three tricks of prevention have purchased them since a credit to admiration: they cannot deny this; and yet now they hate me, and why? because I am excellent; and for no other vile reason on the earth.

E. KNOW. This is strange and barbarous, as ever I heard.

BOB. Nay, for a more instance of their preposterous natures; but note, sir. They have assaulted me some three, four, five, six of them together, as I have walked alone in divers skirts i' the town, as Turnbull, Whitechapel, Shoreditch, which were then my quarters; and since, upon the Exchange, at my lodging, and at my ordinary: where I have driven them afore me the whole length of a street, in the open view of all our gallants, pitying to hurt them, believe me. Yet all this lenity will not overcome their spleen; they will be raising a hill a man may spurn abroad with his foot at pleasure. By myself, I could have slain them all, but I delight not in murder. I am loth to bear any other than this bastinado for them: yet I hold it good polity not to go disarmed, for though I be skilful, I may be oppressed with multitudes.

E. KNOW. Ay, believe me, may you, sir: and in my conceit, our whole nation should sustain the loss by it, if it were so.

BOB. Alas, no? what's a peculiar man to a nation? not seen.

E. KNOW. O, but your skill, sir.

BOB. Indeed, that might be some loss; but who respects it? I will tell you, sir, by the way of private, and under seal; I am a gentleman, and live here obscure, and to myself; but were I known to her majesty and the lords,—observe me,—I would undertake, upon this poor head and life, for the public benefit of the state, not only to spare the entire lives of her subjects in general; but to save the one half, nay, three parts of her yearly charge in holding war, and against what enemy soever. And how would I do it, think you?

E. KNOW. Nay, I know not, nor can I conceive.

BOB. Why thus, sir. I would select nineteen more, to myself,
throughout the land; gentlemen they should be of good spirit,
strong and able constitution; I would choose them by an in-
stinct, a character that I have: and I would teach these nineteen
the special rules, as your punto, your reverso, your stoccata,
your imbroccato, your passada, your montanto; till they could
all play very near, or altogether as well as myself. This done,
say the enemy were forty thousand strong, we twenty would
come into the field the tenth of March, or thereabouts; and we
would challenge twenty of the enemy; they could not in their
honour refuse us: Well, we would kill them; challenge twenty
more, kill them; twenty more, kill them; twenty more, kill
them too; and thus would we kill every man his twenty a day,
that's twenty score; twenty score that's two hundred; two
hundred a day, five days a thousand: forty thousand; forty
times five, five times forty, two hundred days kills them all up
by computation. And this will I venture my poor gentlemanlike
carcase to perform, provided there be no treason practised
upon us, by fair and discreet manhood; that is, civilly by the
sword.

E. KNOW. Why, are you so sure of your hand, captain, at all
times?

BOB. Tut! never miss thrust, upon my reputation with you.

E. KNOW. I would not stand in Downright's state then, an you
meet him, for the wealth of any one street in London.

BOB. Why, sir, you mistake me: if he were here now, by this
welkin, I would not draw my weapon on him. Let this gentleman do his mind: but I will bastinado him, by the bright sun,
wherever I meet him.

MAT. Faith, and I'll have a fling at him, at my distance.

E. KNOW. 'Od's, so, look where he is! yonder he goes.

[DOWNRIGHT *crosses the stage.*

DOW. What peevish luck have I, I cannot meet with these brag-
ging rascals?

BOB. It is not he, is it?

E. KNOW. Yes, faith, it is he.

MAT. I'll be hang'd then if that were he.

E. KNOW. Sir, keep your hanging good for some greater matter, for I assure you that were he.

STEP. Upon my reputation, it was he.

BOB. Had I thought it had been he, he must not have gone so: but I can hardly be induced to believe it was he yet.

E. KNOW. That I think, sir.

Re-enter DOWNRIGHT

But see, he is come again.

DOW. O, Pharaoh's foot, have I found you? Come, draw to your tools; draw, gipsy, or I'll thrash you.

BOB. Gentleman of valour, I do believe in thee; hear me—

DOW. Draw your weapon then.

BOB. Tall man, I never thought on it till now—Body of me, I had a warrant of the peace served on me, even now as I came along, by a water-bearer; this gentleman saw it, Master Mathew.

DOW. 'Sdeath! you will not draw then?

　　　　　　　　　　　[*Disarms and beats him.* MATHEW *runs away.*

BOB. Hold, hold! under thy favour forbear!

DOW. Prate again, as you like this, you whoreson foist you! You'll control the point, you! Your consort is gone; had he staid he had shared with you, sir.　　　　　　　　　　　[*Exit.*

BOB. Well, gentlemen, bear witness, I was bound to the peace, by this good day.

E. KNOW. No, faith, it's an ill day, captain, never reckon it other: but, say you were bound to the peace, the law allows you to defend yourself: that will prove but a poor excuse.

BOB. I cannot tell, sir; I desire good construction in fair sort. I never sustain'd the like disgrace, by heaven! sure I was struck with a planet thence, for I had no power to touch my weapon.

E. KNOW. Ay, like enough; I have heard of many that have been beaten under a planet: go, get you to a surgeon. 'Slid! an these be your tricks, your passadoes, and your montantos, I'll none of them. [*Exit* BOBADILL.] O, manners! that this age should bring forth such creatures! that nature should be at leisure to make them! Come, coz.

POINTS FOR DISCUSSION

1. What terms are used in Scene I which were fashionable at the time when the play was written but which have since dropped out of use? What purpose do these terms serve in the dialogue?

2. What is the source of Mathew's interest in Bobadill?—and of Bobadill's in Mathew?

3. Boasters are characters common enough in literature. What has made Bobadill a famous boaster throughout three centuries? With which other boasters can he be compared?

4. What is Master Stephen's 'humour'? How is it made ridiculous?

5. Discuss the function of the comments made on Bobadill's boastful tales by (*a*) Edward Knowell and Wellbred; (*b*) Mathew and Stephen.

6. Why is it particularly appropriate that Bobadill's plan to win a war by duelling should be put forward at the beginning of Scene III?

7. The Comedy of Humours has been called 'unsympathetic'. Discuss incidents in the play which illustrate this statement.

THE COMEDY OF MANNERS

The figures in Ben Jonson's plays were funny because they had a twist in their characters which made them odd. This twist or 'humour' was part of themselves, and was independent of their social position and of the time at which they happened to live. There have been blunt hearty men, misers, and mockers in all classes and in every age. But the dramatists of the Restoration Period in England laughed at men not so much for their characters as for the way in which they expressed their characters; not for what they were, but for what they did; not for themselves, but for their manners. It was this which gave the name 'Comedy of Manners' to these plays. The people in Restoration Comedies live in a society which obeys very definite rules and follows well-ordered conventions. There are fashions in behaviour just as there are fashions in dress, and it is at these fashions of behaviour that the writers of the Comedies of Manners poke fun. Shakespeare had anticipated the method by making Hamlet laugh at the artificial deference of Osric and his elaborate method of making a simple statement; writers like Congreve laughed at the way wives treated their husbands, or at the trivial round of social observances and idle gossip with which people of good sense were sometimes content to occupy their time.

Before you can enjoy a comedy which pokes fun at manners, it is necessary to have some knowledge of the manners at which fun is being poked. A comedy of manners was interesting only to those audiences who themselves lived among people who behaved rather like the men and women whom they saw in the play. It was not the kind of drama which every one could enjoy, and it flourished at a time when the theatre was attended by the upper classes rather than by the middle classes. A small group of people like those who made up the audiences of the Restoration theatres can have manners and social conventions which differ considerably from those of the ordinary people. When these manners are exaggerated into comedy on the stage, they can become amazingly different from those which are accepted in ordinary life. This has happened with some of the Restoration Comedies, which are like a world on their own, with moral standards quite apart from those which were accepted by the majority of the people at the time when the plays were written and performed.

The best of all the Restoration Comedies is Congreve's *The Way of the World*. The plot is rather complicated, but the chief concern is the pursuit of Millamant by her lover, Mirabell. The scenes chosen show part of the courtship, and the proposal.

THE WAY OF THE WORLD
By WILLIAM CONGREVE

SCENE I

MIRABELL, MRS.[1] MILLAMANT, MRS. FAINALL, WITWOUD, MINCING

MIRA. Here she comes i' faith full Sail, with her Fan spread and
Streamers out, and a Shoal of Fools for Tenders—Ha, no, I
cry her Mercy.

MRS. FAIN. I see but one poor empty Sculler; and he tows her
Woman after him.

MIRA. You seem to be unattended, Madam,—You us'd to have
the *Beau-monde* Throng after you; and a Flock of gay fine
Perukes hovering round you.

WIT. Like Moths about a Candle—I had like to have lost my
Comparison for want of Breath.

MILLA. O I have deny'd my self Airs to Day. I have walk'd as
fast through the Croud—

WIT. As a Favourite just disgrac'd; and with as few Followers.

MILLA. Dear Mr. Witwoud, Truce with your Similitudes: For
I am as Sick of 'em—

WIT. As a Physician of a good Air—I cannot help it, Madam, tho'
'tis against my self.

MILLA. Yet again! Mincing, stand between me and his Wit.

WIT. Do, Mrs. Mincing, like a Skreen before a great Fire. I
confess I do blaze to Day, I am too bright.

MRS. FAIN. But dear Millamant, why were you so long?

MILLA. Long! Lord, have I not made violent haste? I have ask'd
every living Thing I met for you; I have enquir'd after you, as
after a new Fashion.

WIT. Madam, Truce with your Similitudes—No, you met her
Husband, and did not ask him for her.

MIRA. By your leave, Witwoud, that were like enquiring after an
old Fashion, to ask a Husband for his Wife.

WIT. Hum, a hit, a hit, a palpable hit, I confess it.

[1] The term 'Mrs.' was applied to unmarried as well as to married women,
and is pronounced 'Mistress'.

MRS. FAIN. You were dress'd before I came abroad.

MILLA. Ay, that's true—O but then I had—Mincing, what had I? Why was I so long?

MINC. O Mem, your Laship staid to peruse a Pacquet of Letters.

MILLA. O ay, Letters—I had Letters—I am persecuted with Letters—I hate Letters—No Body knows how to write Letters; and yet one has 'em, one does not know why—They serve one to pin up one's Hair.

WIT. Is that the way? Pray, Madam, do you pin up your Hair with all your Letters; I find I must keep Copies.

MILLA. Only with those in Verse, Mr. Witwoud. I never pin up my Hair with Prose. I think I try'd once, Mincing.

MINC. O Mem, I shall never forget it.

MILLA. Ay, poor Mincing tift and tift all the Morning.

MINC. 'Till I had the Cramp in my Fingers, I'll vow, Mem. And all to no purpose. But when your Laship pins it up with Poetry, it sits so pleasant the next Day as any Thing, and is so pure and so crips.

WIT. Indeed, so crips?

MINC. You're such a Critick, Mr. Witwoud.

MILLA. Mirabell, Did you take Exceptions last Night? O ay, and went away—Now I think on't I'm angry—No, now I think on't I'm pleas'd—for I believe I gave you some Pain.

MIRA. Does that please you?

MILLA. Infinitely; I love to give Pain.

MIRA. You wou'd affect a Cruelty which is not in your Nature; your true Vanity is in the Power of pleasing.

MILLA. O I ask your Pardon for that—Ones Cruelty is ones Power, and when one parts with ones Cruelty, one parts with ones Power; and when one has parted with that, I fancy one's old and ugly.

MIRA. Ay, ay, suffer your Cruelty to ruin the Object of your Power, to destroy your Lover—And then how vain, how lost a Thing you'll be? Nay, 'tis true: You are no longer handsome when you've lost your Lover; your Beauty dies upon the Instant: For Beauty is the Lover's Gift; 'tis he bestows your

Charms—Your Glass is all a Cheat. The Ugly and the Old, whom the Looking-glass mortifies, yet after Commendation can be flatter'd by it, and discover Beauties in it: For that reflects our Praises, rather than your Face.

MILLA. O the Vanity of these Men! Fainall, d'ye hear him? If they did not commend us, we were not handsome! Now you must know they cou'd not commend one, if one was not handsome. Beauty the Lover's Gift—Lord, what is a Lover, that it can give? Why, one makes Lovers as fast as one pleases, and they live as long as one pleases, and they die as soon as one pleases: And then if one pleases one makes more.

WIT. Very pretty. Why, you make no more of making of Lovers, Madam, than of making so many Card-matches.

MILLA. One no more owes ones Beauty to a Lover, than ones Wit to an Eccho: They can but reflect what we look and say; vain empty Things if we are silent or unseen, and want a Being.

MIRA. Yet, to those two vain empty Things, you owe two of the greatest Pleasures of your Life.

MILLA. How so?

MIRA. To your Lover you owe the Pleasure of hearing your selves prais'd; and to an Eccho the Pleasure of hearing your selves talk.

WIT. But I know a Lady that loves Talking so incessantly, she won't give an Eccho fair play; and she has that everlasting Rotation of Tongue, that an Eccho must wait 'till she dies, before it can catch her last Words.

MILLA. O Fiction; Fainall, let us leave these Men.

SCENE II

MILLAMANT, MIRABELL

MIRA. *Like* Daphne *she, as Lovely and as Coy.* Do you lock your self up from me, to make my Search more curious? Or is this pretty Artifice contriv'd, to signifie that here the Chace must end, and my Pursuit be crown'd, for you can fly no further?

MILLA. Vanity! No—I'll fly and be follow'd to the last Moment, tho' I am upon the very Verge of Matrimony, I expect you

　　　should sollicit me as much as if I were wavering at the Grate
　　　of a Monastery, with one Foot over the Threshold. I'll be
　　　sollicited to the very last, nay and afterwards.

MIRA. What, after the last?

MILLA. O, I should think I was poor and had nothing to bestow,
　　　if I were reduc'd to an inglorious Ease; and freed from the
　　　agreeable Fatigues of Sollicitation.

MIRA. But do not you know, that when Favours are conferr'd
　　　upon instant and tedious Sollicitation, that they diminish in
　　　their Value, and that both the Giver loses the Grace, and the
　　　Receiver lessens his Pleasure?

MILLA. It may be in Things of common Application; but never
　　　sure in Love. O, I hate a Lover, that can dare to think he
　　　draws a Moment's Air, independent on the Bounty of his
　　　Mistress. There is not so impudent a Thing in Nature, as the
　　　sawcy Look of an assured Man, confident of Success. The
　　　Pedantick Arrogance of a very Husband, has not so Pragmatical
　　　an Air. Ah! I'll never marry, unless I am first made sure of
　　　my Will and Pleasure.

MIRA. Would you have 'em both before Marriage? Or will you
　　　be contented with the first now, and stay for the other 'till after
　　　Grace?

MILLA. Ah don't be impertinent—My dear Liberty, shall I leave
　　　thee? My faithful Solitude, my darling Contemplation, must
　　　I bid you then Adieu? Ay-h adieu—My Morning Thoughts,
　　　agreeable Wakings, indolent Slumbers, all ye *douceurs*, ye
　　　Sommeils du Matin, adieu—I can't do't, 'tis more than impossible
　　　—Positively Mirabell, I'll lye a-bed in a Morning as long as I
　　　please.

MIRA. Then I'll get up in a Morning as early as I please.

MILLA. Ah! Idle Creature, get up when you will—And d'ye
　　　hear, I won't be call'd Names after I'm Marry'd; positively
　　　I won't be call'd Names.

MIRA. Names!

MILLA. Ay, as Wife, Spouse, my Dear, Joy. Jewel, Love, Sweet-
　　　heart, and the rest of that nauseous Cant, in which Men and

their Wives are so fulsomly familiar,—I shall never bear that —Good Mirabell don't let us be familiar or fond, nor kiss before Folks, like my Lady Fadler and Sir Francis: Nor go to Hide-Park together the first Sunday in a new Chariot, to provoke Eyes and Whispers; And then never be seen there together again; as if we were proud of one another the first Week, and asham'd of one another ever after. Let us never Visit together, nor go to a Play together, but let us be very strange and well bred: Let us be as strange as if we had been marry'd a great while; and as well bred as if we were not marry'd at all.

MIRA. Have you any more Conditions to offer? Hitherto your Demands are pretty reasonable.

MILLA. Trifles,—As Liberty to pay and receive Visits to and from whom I please; to write and receive Letters, without Interrogatories or wry Faces on your part; to wear what I please; and chuse Conversation with regard only to my own Taste; to have no Obligation upon me to converse with Wits that I don't like, because they are your Acquaintance; or to be intimate with Fools, because they may be your Relations. Come to Dinner when I please, dine in my Dressing-Room when I'm out of Humour, without giving a Reason. To have my Closet inviolate; to be sole Empress of my Tea-Table, which you must never presume to approach without first asking leave. And lastly, where-ever I am, you shall always knock at the Door before you come in. These Articles subscrib'd, if I continue to endure you a little longer, I may by degrees dwindle into a Wife.

MIRA. Your Bill of Fare is something advanc'd in this latter Account. Well, have I Liberty to offer Conditions—That when you are dwindled into a Wife, I may not be beyond measure enlarg'd into a Husband.

MILLA. You have free leave, propose your utmost, speak and spare not.

MIRA. I thank you. *Inprimis* then, I covenant that your Acquaintance be general; that you admit no sworn Confident, or Intimate of your own Sex; no she Friend to skreen her Affairs under your Countenance, and tempt you to make Trial of a mutual Secresie. No Decoy-Duck to wheadle you a *fop*—*scrambling* to the Play in a Mask—Then bring you home in a pretended Fright, when you think you shall be found out—And rail at me for missing the Play, and disappointing the Frolick which you had to pick me up and prove my Constancy.

MILLA. Detestable *Inprimis*! I go to the Play in a Mask!

MIRA. *Item*, I Article, that you continue to like your own Face, as long as I shall: And while it passes current with me, that you endeavour not to new Coin it. To which end, together with all Vizards for the Day, I prohibit all Masks for the Night, made of Oil'd-skins and I know not what—Hog's Bones, Hare's Gall, Pig Water, and the Marrow of a roasted Cat. In short, I forbid all Commerce with the Gentlewoman in *what-d'ye-call-it* Court. *Item*, I shut my Doors against all Maids with Baskets, and penny-worths of *Muslin, China, Fans, Atlasses, &c.—Item*, when you shall be Breeding——

MILLA. Ah! Name it not.

MIRA. Which may be presum'd, with a Blessing on our Endeavours—

MILLA. Odious Endeavours!

MIRA. I denounce against all strait Lacing, squeezing for a Shape, 'till you mould my Boy's Head like a Sugar-loaf; and instead of a Man-Child, make me Father to a Crooked-billet. Lastly, to the Dominion of the *Tea-Table* I submit.—But with *proviso*, that you exceed not in your Province; but restrain your self to native and simple *Tea-Table* drinks, as *Tea, Chocolate*, and *Coffee*. As likewise to Genuine and Authoriz'd *Tea-Table* Talk—Such as mending of Fashions, spoiling Reputations, railing at absent Friends, and so forth—But that on no Account you encroach upon the Mens Prerogative, and presume to drink Healths, or toast Fellows; for prevention of which, I banish all *Foreign Forces*, all Auxiliaries to the *Tea-Table*, as *Orange-Brandy*, all *Anniseed, Cinamon, Citron*, and *Barbado's-Waters*, together with *Ratafia*, and the most noble Spirit of *Clary*.—But for *Couslip-Wine, Poppy-Water*, and all

Dormitives, those I allow.—These *Proviso's* admitted, in other things I may prove a tractable and complying Husband.

MILLA. O horrid *Proviso's*! Filthy strong Waters! I toast Fellows, Odious Men! I hate your odious *Proviso's*.

MIRA. Then we're agreed. Shall I kiss your Hand upon the Contract? and here comes one to be a Witness to the Sealing of the Deed.

SCENE III

(*To them*) MRS. FAINALL

MILLA. Fainall, what shall I do? Shall I have him? I think I must have him.

MRS. FAIN. Ay, ay, take him, take him, what shou'd you do?

MILLA. Well then—I'll take my Death I'm in a horrid Fright— Fainall, I shall never say it—Well—I think—I'll endure you.

MRS. FAIN. Fy, fy, have him, have him, and tell him so in plain Terms: For I am sure you have a Mind to him.

MILLA. Are you? I think I have—and the horrid Man looks as if he thought so too—Well, you ridiculous thing you, I'll have you—I won't be kiss'd, nor I won't be thank'd—Here kiss my Hand tho'—So, hold your Tongue now, don't say a Word.

MRS. FAIN. Mirabell, there's a Necessity for your Obedience;— You have neither time to talk nor stay. My Mother is coming; and in my Conscience if she shou'd see you, wou'd fall into Fits, and may be not recover, time enough to return to Sir Rowland; who, as Foible tells me, is in a fair Way to succeed. Therefore spare your Extacies for another Occasion, and slip down the back Stairs, where Foible waits to consult you.

MILLA. Ay; go, go. In the mean time I suppose you have said something to please me.

MIRA. I am all Obedience.

POINTS FOR DISCUSSION

1. 'His personages are a kind of intellectual gladiators; every sentence is to ward or strike' (Dr. Johnson). Find examples of this from Scene I. Which examples do you consider the best?

2. How can you show that, in the proposal scene, it is taken for granted that Millamant is in love with Mirabell?

3. What is it about marriage which is making Millamant hesitate to accept Mirabell?

4. The characters of Congreve's plays have sometimes been criticized as heartless creatures, concerned merely with expressing themselves as brilliantly as possible. Does this seem to be true of Millamant?

5. How do you think the lines of this play ought to be spoken? Compare them in this respect with the speeches in *Dr. Faustus* and with those in *Strife*.

CHAPTER V

SENTIMENT AND MELODRAMA

THE PLAYS OF SENTIMENT

COMEDIES like those of Congreve showed people their every-day lives, idealized and made more vivid, it is true, but still having obvious links with the world of ordinary experience. People went to the theatre to see themselves in a new light. But they also wanted, on occasions, to be 'taken out of them-selves' and to be shown a world which was not limited by the petty restraints of conventional social existence. The plays which met this need were known as 'heroic dramas'—'heroic' because the characters were of a larger mould and moved in an ampler world than that of ordinary experience. The difficulty of a dramatist who leaves the world of reality is to know how far he may go in the world of imagination without becoming absurd. In the opinion of later genera-tions, the dramatists of this period went much too far away from possibility in their desire to create a world of super-men, and the deeds of valour done by the heroes of these plays were as fantastic as those of Puss in Boots or of Tom Thumb, who was chosen as the hero of a burlesque tragedy of this kind by Henry Fielding, *The Tragedy of Tragedies, or Tom Thumb the Great.*

In the eighteenth century, middle-class people began to go to the theatre, and this new audience demanded new plays. They were unwilling to see the Restoration Comedies, which had moral standards utterly different from their own, especially as they had been warned against such plays by Jeremy Collier in his *Short View of the Immorality and Profaneness of the English Stage.* The heroic dramas did not stir their hearts, because they found it impossible to understand heroes of such absurd magnitude of character. They wanted plays of a different type: plays which should, in the first place, appear to be highly respectable; and, in the second place, contain characters with whose thoughts they could sympathize and whose emotions they could share. Their favourite emotion was pity, a feeling of tender solicitude for the misfortunes of the characters in the play, who spent much of their time uttering lofty thoughts called 'sentiments'. There were no villains in these plays, for the villain of the first four acts always reformed in the fifth and brought tears from the audience by an overwhelming repentance for his past misdeeds. The success of the dramatist depended largely on his ability to bring his characters into situations in which their tender feelings should be so distressed that the audience might weep in sympathy for them. These plays included both comedies and tragedies. Most of the tragedies of this type no longer had kings and princes for their heroes; instead, they had everyday characters—the kind of people with whom members of the audience were familiar in their ordinary lives.

Of this kind was *The London Merchant, or the History of George Barnwell*, a play which created a great stir when it was first produced, and became the most popular of all the tragedies of this type. George Barnwell and his companion, Trueman, are apprenticed to Thorowgood, a wealthy London Merchant, who is an altogether admirable master. Maria, Thorowgood's daughter, is secretly in love with Barnwell, who would eventually have been able to marry her. Into this scene of domestic happiness and good fortune comes Millwood, who stops Barnwell in the street one day, and lures him to her home on the pretext of having some news of moment to impart to him. He falls in love with her and becomes her slave. She induces him to steal money from his master until, tormented by his conscience, he dares no longer return to him. He quits Thorowgood's house, leaving a note for his friend Trueman confessing that he has embezzled his master's money. Trueman reads this note to Maria, who offers to make good the money from her private fortune if Trueman will conceal the theft from her father. But Lucy, Millwood's servant, confesses to Thorowgood that her mistress has induced Barnwell to embezzle Thorowgood's money; and tells him further that the latest plot is for Barnwell to murder and rob his uncle. As soon as he hears this, Thorowgood orders a horse, and gallops off to avert the catastrophe. Meanwhile, George Barnwell has set off to do the deed, and Thorowgood arrives too late.

THE LONDON MERCHANT

OR

THE HISTORY OF GEORGE BARNWELL

By GEORGE LILLO

SCENE I. *A walk at some distance from a Country-Seat*

BARNWELL

BARN. A dismal gloom obscures the face of day. Either the sun has slipped behind a cloud, or journeys down the west of heaven with more than common speed, to avoid the sight of what I am doomed to act. Since I set forth on this accursed design, where'er I tread, methinks the solid earth trembles beneath my feet. Yonder limpid stream, whose hoary fall has made a natural cascade, as I passed by, in doleful accents seemed to murmur 'Murder!' The earth, the air and water seem concerned, but that's not strange: the world is punished, and Nature feels the shock, when Providence permits a good man's fall. Just Heaven! Then what should I be! For him that was my father's only brother—and, since his death, has been to me a father; who took me up an infant and an orphan, reared me with tenderest care, and still indulged me with most paternal fondness? Yet here I stand avowed his destined murderer—I stiffen with horror at my own impiety. 'Tis yet unperformed—what if I quit my bloody purpose, and fly the place? [*Going, then stops.*] But whither, oh, whither shall I fly? My master's once friendly doors are ever shut against me; and without money Millwood will never see me more; and life is not to be endured without her. She's got such firm possession of my heart and governs there with such despotic sway.—Ay, there's the cause of all my sin and sorrow: 'tis more than love; 'tis the fever of the soul and madness of desire. In vain does nature, reason, conscience, all oppose it; the impetuous passion bears down all before it, and drives me on to lust, to theft, and murder. Oh, conscience! feeble guide to virtue! who only shows us when we go astray, but wants the power to stop us in our course!—Ha! in yonder shady walk I see my uncle. He's alone. Now for my disguise. [*Plucks out a visor.*] This is his hour of private meditation. Thus daily he prepares his soul for Heaven; whilst I—But what have I to do with Heaven? Ha! no struggles, conscience—

Hence, hence, remorse, and ev'ry thought that's good:
The storm that lust began must end in blood.

[*Puts on the visor, draws a pistol (and exit).*]

SCENE II. *A close walk in a Wood*

UNCLE

UNCLE. If I were superstitious, I should fear some danger lurked unseen, or death were nigh. A heavy melancholy clouds my spirits. My imagination is filled with ghastly forms of dreary graves, and bodies changed by death; when the pale lengthened visage attracts each weeping eye, and fills the musing soul at once with grief and horror, pity and aversion.—I will indulge the thought. The wise man prepares himself for death by making it familiar to his mind. When strong reflections hold the mirror near, and the living in the dead behold their future selves, how does each inordinate passion and desire cease, or sicken at the view! The mind scarce moves; the blood, curdling and chilled, creeps slowly through the veins: fixed still, and motionless like the solemn object of our thoughts, we are almost at present what we must be hereafter; till curiosity awakes the soul, and sets it on inquiry.

SCENE III

UNCLE, GEORGE BARNWELL *at a distance*

UNCLE. O Death! thou strange mysterious power, seen every day, yet never understood but by the incommunicative dead, what art thou? The extensive mind of man, that with a thought circles the earth's vast globe, sinks to the centre, or ascends above the stars; that worlds exotic finds, or thinks it finds, thy thick clouds attempts to pass in vain, lost and bewildered in the horrid gloom; defeated, she returns more doubtful than before; of nothing certain but of labour lost.

[*During this speech* BARNWELL *sometimes presents the pistol, and draws it back again; at last he drops it, at which his* UNCLE *starts and draws his sword.*

BARN. Oh, 'tis impossible!

UNCLE. A man so near me! armed and masked—

BARN. Nay, then there's no retreat.

[*Plucks a poignard from his bosom, and stabs him.*

UNCLE. Oh, I am slain! All-gracious Heaven, regard the prayer of thy dying servant; bless, with thy choicest blessings, my dearest nephew; forgive my murderer, and take my fleeting soul to endless mercy.

[BARNWELL *throws off his mask; runs to him; and kneeling by him, raises and chafes him.*

BARN. Expiring saint! Oh, murdered, martyred uncle! lift up your dying eyes, and view your nephew in your murderer!— Oh, do not look so tenderly upon me!—Let indignation lighten from your eyes, and blast me ere you die!—By Heaven, he weeps, in pity of my woes!—Tears, tears, for blood!—The murdered, in the agonies of death, weeps for his murderer.— Oh, speak your pious purpose; pronounce my pardon, then, and take me with you!—He would, but cannot.—Oh, why, with such fond affection, do you press my murdering hand?— What! will you kiss me? [*Kisses him.* UNCLE *groans and dies.*] He is gone for ever—and oh! I follow. [*Swoons away upon his* UNCLE'S *dead body.*] Do I still live to press the suffering bosom of the earth? Do I still breathe, and taint with my infectious breath the wholesome air? Let Heaven from its high throne, in justice or in mercy, now look down on that dear murdered saint, and me the murderer. And, if his vengeance spares, let pity strike and end my wretched being!—Murder the worst of crimes, and parricide the worst of murders, and this the worst of parricides! Cain, who stands on record from the birth of time, and must to its last final period, as accursed, slew a brother favoured above him. Detested Nero by another's hand dispatched a mother that he feared and hated. But I, with my own hand, have murdered a brother, mother, father, and a friend, most loving and beloved. This execrable act of mine's without a parallel. O may it ever stand alone—the last of murders, as it is the worst!

The rich man thus, in torment and despair,
Preferred his vain, but charitable prayer.
The fool, his own soul lost, would fain be wise
For others' good; but Heaven his suit denies.
By laws and means well known we stand or fall,
And one eternal rule remains for all.

> [*When* BARNWELL *returned to* MILLWOOD *after the murder, she betrayed him, and he was arrested. Later,* MILLWOOD *was arrested on the accusation of* THOROWGOOD.]

SCENE IV

BARNWELL (*in the condemned cell*)

BARN. Vain, busy thoughts, be still! What avails it to think on what I might have been? I now am what I've made myself.

To him TRUEMAN *and* MARIA

TRUE. Madam, reluctant I lead you to this dismal scene. This is the seat of misery and guilt. Here awful justice reserves her public victims. This is the entrance to shameful death.

MARIA. To this sad place, then, no improper guest, the abandoned, lost Maria brings despair—and see the subject and the cause of all this world of woe! Silent and motionless he stands, as if his soul had quitted her abode, and the lifeless form alone was left behind—yet that so perfect that beauty and death, ever at enmity, now seem united there.

BARN. I groan, but murmur not. Just Heaven, I am your own; do with me what you please.

MARIA. Why are your streaming eyes still fixed below, as though thou didst give the greedy earth thy sorrows, and rob me of my due? Were happiness within your power, you should bestow it where you pleased; but in your misery I must and will partake!

BARN. Oh! say not so, but fly, abhor, and leave me to my fate! Consider what you are—how vast your fortune, and how bright your fame; have pity on your youth, your beauty, and unequalled virtue, for which so many noble peers have sighed in vain! Bless with your charms some honourable lord! Adorn with your beauty, and by your example improve, the English Court, that justly claims such merit: so shall I quickly be to you as though I had never been.

MARIA. When I forget you, I must be so indeed. Reason, choice, virtue, all forbid it. Let women, like Millwood, if there be more such women, smile in prosperity, and in adversity forsake! Be it the pride of virtue to repair, or to partake, the ruin such have made.

TRUE. Lovely, ill-fated maid! Was there ever such generous distress before? How must this pierce his grateful heart, and aggravate his woes!

BARN. Ere I knew guilt or shame—when fortune smiled, and when my youthful hopes were at the highest—if then to have raised my thoughts to you, had been presumption in me, never to have been pardoned: think how much beneath yourself you condescend, to regard me now!

MARIA. Let her blush, who, professing love, invades the freedom of your sex's choice, and meanly sues in hopes of a return! Your inevitable fate hath rendered hope impossible as vain. Then, why should I fear to avow a passion so just and so disinterested?

TRUE. If any should take occasion, from Millwood's crimes, to libel the best and fairest part of the creation, here let them see their error! The most distant hopes of such a tender passion from so bright a maid add to the happiness of the most happy, and make the greatest proud. Yet here 'tis lavished in vain: though by the rich present the generous donor is undone, he on whom it is bestowed receives no benefit.

BARN. So the aromatic spices of the East, which all the living covet and esteem, are, with unavailing kindness, wasted on the dead.

MARIA. Yes, fruitless is my love, and unavailing all my sighs and tears. Can they save thee from approaching death—from such a death? Oh, terrible idea! What is her misery and distress, who sees the first last object of her love, for whom alone she'd live—for whom she'd die a thousand, thousand deaths, if it were possible—expiring in her arms? Yet she is happy, when compared to me. Were millions of worlds mine, I'd gladly give them in exchange for her condition. The most consummate woe is light to mine. The last of curses to other miserable maids is all I ask; and that's denied me.

TRUE. Time and reflections cure all ills.

MARIA. All but this; his dreadful catastrophe virtue herself abhors. To give a holiday to suburb slaves, and passing entertain the savage herd, who, elbowing each other for a sight, pursue and press upon him like his fate! A mind with piety and resolution armed may smile on death. But public ignominy, everlasting shame—shame, the death of souls—to die a thousand times, and yet survive even death itself, in never-dying infamy—is this to be endured? Can I who live in him, and must, each hour of my devoted life, feel all these woes renewed, can I endure this?

TRUE. Grief has impaired her spirits; she pants as in the agonies of death.

BARN. Preserve her, Heaven, and restore her peace; nor let her death be added to my crime! [*Bell tolls.*] I am summoned to my fate.

SCENE XI

To them, KEEPER

KEEPER. The officers attend you, sir. Mrs. Millwood is already summoned.

BARN. Tell 'em I am ready. And now, my friend, farewell! [*Embracing.*] Support and comfort the best you can this mourning fair.—No more! Forget not to pray for me! [*Turning to* MARIA.] Would you, bright excellence, permit me the honour of a chaste embrace, the last happiness this world could give were mine. [*She inclines towards him; they embrace.*] Exalted goodness! O turn your eyes from earth, and me, to Heaven, where virtue, like yours, is ever heard. Pray for the peace of my departing soul! Early my race of wickedness began, and soon has reached the summit. Ere Nature has finished her work, and stamped me man—just at the time that others begin to stray—my course is finished. Though short my span of life, and few my days, yet, count my crimes for years, and I have lived whole ages. Justice and mercy are in Heaven the same: its utmost severity is mercy to the whole, thereby to cure man's folly and presumption, which else would render even infinite mercy vain and ineffectual. Thus justice, in compassion to mankind, cuts off a wretch like me, by one such example to secure thousands from future ruin.

If any youth, like you, in future times
Shall mourn my fate, though he abhor my crimes;
Or tender maid, like you, my tale shall hear,
And to my sorrows give a pitying tear;
To each such melting eye, and throbbing heart,

Would gracious Heaven this benefit impart
Never to know my guilt, nor feel my pain:
Then must you own, you ought not to complain:
Since you nor weep, nor shall I die, in vain.

POINTS FOR DISCUSSION

1. Like the soliloquy of Macbeth before he goes to kill Duncan, the opening speech by George Barnwell is an attempt to represent the thoughts of a man immediately before he becomes a murderer. Why does Barnwell's speech seem so much less real than Macbeth's, even though Macbeth speaks in verse and Barnwell in prose?

2. Is it probable that Barnwell's uncle would have thought of *ghastly forms of dreary graves* as he was walking in his garden? Why are such thoughts put into his soliloquy?

3. What is meant by saying that a play is 'undramatic'? Give illustrations from this play.

4. In the characters of Shakespeare's heroes there is a contrast, but in the character of George Barnwell there is a flat contradiction. What is it?

5. There are one or two passages of verse in the play. What is their purpose?

6. When plays of a kind similar to this were recently acted in London, most of the audience regarded them as burlesques. What is meant by 'burlesque drama'? Why would this play be easy to burlesque?

MELODRAMA AND NATURALISM

In the second half of the eighteenth century, the popularity of the sentimental plays declined. Their place was taken by the vigorous comedies of Sheridan and Goldsmith, which, without the extreme artificiality of the earlier plays, had many resemblances to the Comedy of Manners of the Restoration. And then, quite suddenly, dramas of permanent interest ceased to be written. The comedies of Goldsmith and Sheridan stand like a little oasis, with the artificial sentimental plays behind them, and a hundred years of dramatic drought in front.

Many suggestions have been made to account for this

sudden decline in the writing of plays. It has been maintained that the great writers of the period were interested in themselves and their own thoughts and emotions, and valued these thoughts and emotions in proportion as they found them individual and personal. A dramatist must use his own thoughts as a means of understanding the thoughts of other people. He must look outside himself, and writers like Wordsworth, Shelley, and Byron were interested in events outside themselves only for the sake of the reflection which these events made in their own minds.

A more obvious reason for the decline in productions for the theatres can be found in the conditions which existed in the theatres themselves. At that time, only four theatres in London were licensed to produce plays: Drury Lane, Covent Garden, His Majesty's, and the Haymarket. To make the fullest use of their monopoly, they were greatly increased in size. These huge buildings made the same demands upon the actors as had been made by the Greek theatres. It became necessary to exaggerate. The English actors did not take to wearing the buskins and masks of the Greeks, but they had to develop a powerful and declamatory manner of speaking, and emphasize their words with extravagant gestures. Greek plays had been written for the theatre in which they were acted, but most English plays had been written for an entirely different type of theatre, and their appeal was destroyed when they were acted in this highly artificial way. The dramatists of the time were not sufficiently interested in the theatre to be prepared to develop a new type of drama which would be adapted to this new kind of building, and the managers of the theatres found that the eye could bridge distances better than the ear. The theatres became places of a form of entertainment which was not essentially dramatic. Elaborate pageants were introduced, and scenic displays of all kinds, which often crowded the drama itself into insignificance. When they went to the theatre, people ceased to be interested in drama which would interpret human experience or introduce them to new personalities. They expected to be entertained and diverted with surprising scenic effects set in a framework of drama which sacrificed truth to sensationalism.

The Licensing Act which made the regular theatres increase the size of their buildings had also another effect. Small 'pirate' theatres were built all round London which had to create the legal fiction that they were not theatres at all, but places of entertainment of a different kind. The managers of these minor theatres pretended that they were producing, not plays, but operas and musical pieces. The plays themselves were altered often beyond recognition, and cut short so that they could be interspersed with songs and odd pieces of entertainment of all kinds. As well as thrusting musical 'turns' in between dramatic pieces, managers introduced music into the plays themselves by announcing the entrance of the characters with an appropriate tune. This proved very popular. The audiences developed a taste for plays with well-marked and exaggerated characters, and the music told them what to expect. Of these characters it might be said that:

> 'When they were good, they were very very good,
> And when they were bad, they were horrid!'

As low, sinister music announced the approach of the villain, the spectators hissed and booed, but cheered loudly when the hero entered. These audiences certainly enjoyed themselves, although it would be difficult to say that they enjoyed the play, which, as in the regular theatres, became a matter of secondary importance. The plays which were written had more than a little in common with the sentimental plays of the eighteenth century, altered so that they had much less talk and much more action, and portrayed villains who were torn by the pangs of remorse without enjoying the blessings of repentance.

These '*melo*dramas' as they were called (because of the introduction of music as a background to the dialogue) had a long run of popularity. The play which was to mark the end of the old type of melodrama was *Caste*, by T. W. Robertson, which appeared in 1867. The difference between this play and those which were popular at the time lay in the naturalness of the dialogue and situations, which were much closer to those of real life than those in the melodramas. The world is not composed of villains and heroes, but of ordinary men and women who have faults and weaknesses in greater or less degree; and it became the object of dramatists like Robertson to make the audience believe that while they were watching the play they were seeing something which belonged to real life. The advance which Robertson made can be seen by comparing a scene from *Caste* with a scene from one of the best known of the old-time melodramas, *Maria Marten, or the Murder in the Red Barn.*

MARIA MARTEN
OR
THE MURDER IN THE RED BARN

[Corder, the villain, has determined to kill Maria, lest she should reveal that he has murdered their baby. On the pretence that he wishes to take her to London, where they can be married, Corder lures Maria to the Red Barn, whither she goes disguised as a boy.]

INSIDE THE RED BARN

CORDER *discovered digging a grave.* [*Villain's music*]

CORDER. All is complete, I await my victim. Will she come? Oh yes, a woman is fool enough to do anything for the man she loves. Hark, tis her footstep bounding across the fields! She comes, with hope in her heart, a song on her lips, little does she think that death is so near.   [*He steps into a dark corner.*

Enter MARIA [*The music turns soft and gentle*]

MARIA. William not here, where can he be, what ails me? A weight is at my heart as if it told some evil, and this old Barn— how like a vault it looks! Fear steals upon me, I tremble in every limb, I will return to my home at once.

CORDER [*advancing*]. Stay, Maria!

MARIA. I'm glad you are here, you don't know how frightened I've been.

CORDER. Did any one see you cross the fields?

MARIA. Not a soul, I remembered your instructions.

CORDER. That's good. Now, Maria, do you remember a few days ago threatening to betray me about the child to Constable Ayres?   [*Tremolo fiddles.*

MARIA. A girlish threat made in a heat of temper, because you refused to do justice to one you had wronged so greatly. Do not speak of that now, let us leave this place.

CORDER. Not yet Maria, you don't think my life is to be held at the bidding of a silly girl. *No*, look what I have made here!
[*He drags her to the grave. Slow music.*

MARIA. A grave. Oh William, what do you mean?

CORDER. To kill you, bury your body there. You are a clog upon my actions, a chain that keeps me from reaching ambitious height, you are to die.

MARIA [*kneels*]. But not by your hand, the hand that I have clasped in love and confidence. Oh! think, William, how much I have sacrificed for you, think of our little child above, now in heaven, pleads for its mother's life. Oh spare, oh spare me!

CORDER. 'Tis useless, my mind's resolved, you die tonight.
[*Thunder and lightning.*

MARIA. Wretch!

Since neither prayers nor tears will touch your stony heart,
Heaven will surely nerve my arm to battle for my life.
[*She seizes* CORDER.

CORDER. Foolish girl, desist!

MARIA. Never with life!

[*They struggle, he shoots her, she falls in his arms.*

MARIA [*soft music*].

William, I am dying, your cruel hand has stilled
The heart that beat in love alone for thee.
Think not to escape the hand of justice, for
When least expected it will mark you down,
At that moment think of Maria's wrongs.

Death claims me, and with my last breath I die blessing and
forgiving thee. [*Dies.*

CORDER. Blessing and forgiveness! and for me, her [*loud music*]
murderer! What have I done! Oh Maria, awake, awake, do
not look so tenderly upon me, let indignation lighten from your
eyes and blast me!

Oh may this crime for ever stand accurst,
The last of murders, as it is the worst.

CASTE

By T. W. ROBERTSON

THE STORY. The Honourable George D'Alroy, son of the Marquise
de St. Maur, falls in love with Esther Eccles, a ballet dancer, whom
he marries, much against the wishes of Captain Hawtree, his friend,
who is paying his addresses to Lady Florence Carberry. Soon after
the marriage, George is summoned to join his regiment and to go
to India, to help in quelling the Mutiny. News comes that he has
been captured by sepoys and killed, and Esther is compelled to
return to her own family. A baby son is born, whom Esther tries
to rear as well as she can in difficult surroundings. Her father,
Eccles, is a drunken waster; her sister Polly is of the vivacious,
tomboy type, and is engaged to be married to Sam Gerridge, a
plumber and gas-fitter, who very much resents the superior airs
of Captain Hawtree. In order to earn some money, Esther is
planning to return to the stage, and is one day surprised to receive
a visit from her mother-in-law, the Marquise, who wishes to take
her grandson and bring him up in the traditions of her family.

Esther refuses to part with her son, and after the Marquise has gone, Captain Hawtree calls at the house.

SCENE. *A room in a little house in Stangate. The door is right; by it, a piano; the fireplace left; the window, which gives a view of iron railings and a mean street, at back. A long table in middle of room. Sword with crape knot, spurs, and a cap, craped, hanging over chimney-piece. Portrait of D'Alroy (large) on mantelpiece.*

> SAM *and* POLLY *are together, having just informed* ECCLES *of their engagement.* ECCLES *has gone to recover from the shock of the news at the nearest public-house. There is a knock at the door, and* HAWTREE *(now a Major) enters.*

HAWTREE. I met the Marquise's carriage on the bridge. Has she been here?

POLLY. Yes.

HAWTREE. What happened?

POLLY. Oh, she wanted to take away the child.

SAM. In the coach.   [POLLY *sets tea-things.*

HAWTREE. And what did Mrs. D'Alroy say to that?

SAM. Mrs. D'Alroy said that she'd see her blow'd first! or words to that effect.

HAWTREE. I'm sorry to hear this; I had hoped—however, that's over.

POLLY. Yes, it's over; and I hope we shall hear no more about it. Want to take away the child, indeed—like her impudence! What next! Esther's gone to lie down. I shan't wake her up for tea, though she's had nothing to eat all day.

SAM. Shall I fetch some shrimps?

POLLY. No. What made you think of shrimps?

SAM. They're a relish, and consolin'—at least I always found 'em so.

POLLY. I won't ask you to take tea with us, Major—you're too grand.

HAWTREE [*placing hat on piano*]. Not at all. I shall be most happy. [*Aside.*] 'Pon my word, these are very good sort of people. I'd no idea—

SAM. He's a-going to stop to tea—well, I ain't.

> [*Goes up to window and sits.* HAWTREE *crosses and sits right of table.*

POLLY. Sam! Sam! [*Pause. He says 'Eh?'*] Pull down the blind and light the gas.

SAM. No, don't light up; I like this sort of dusk. It's unbusiness-like, but pleasant.

> [SAM *cuts enormous slice of bread, and hands it on point of knife to* HAWTREE. *Cuts small lump of butter, and hands it on point of knife to* HAWTREE, *who looks at it through eye-glass, then takes it.* SAM *then helps himself.* POLLY *meantime has poured out tea in two cups, and one saucer for* SAM, *sugars them, and then hands cup and saucer to* HAWTREE, *who has both hands full. He takes it awkwardly, and places it on table.* POLLY, *having only one spoon, tastes* SAM'S *tea, then stirs* HAWTREE'S, *attracting his attention by so doing. He looks into his tea-cup.* POLLY *stirs her own tea, and drops spoon into* HAWTREE'S *cup, causing it to spurt in his eye. He drops eyeglass and wipes his eyes.*

POLLY [*making tea*]. Sugar, Sam! [SAM *takes tea and sits facing fire*]. Oh, there isn't any milk—it'll be here directly, it's just his time.

VOICE [*outside; rattle of milk-pails*]. Mia-oow!

POLLY. There he is. [*Knock at door.*] Oh, I know; I owe him fourpence. [*Feeling her pockets.*] Sam, have you got fourpence?

> [*Knock again, louder.*

SAM. No [*his mouth full*] I ain't got no fourpence.

POLLY. He's very impatient. Come in!

> [*Enter* GEORGE, *his face bronzed, and in full health. He carries a milk-can in his hand, which, after putting his hat on piano, he places on table.*

GEORGE. A fellow hung this on the railings, so I brought it in.

> [POLLY *sees him, and gradually sinks down under the table, right. Then* SAM, *with his mouth full, and bread and butter in hand, does the same, left.* HAWTREE *pushes himself back a space, in chair, remains motionless.* GEORGE *astonished. Picture.*

GEORGE. What's the matter with you?

HAWTREE [*rising*]. George!

GEORGE. Hawtree! You here?

POLLY [*under table*]. O-o-o-o-oh! the ghost!—the ghost!

SAM. It shan't hurt you, Polly. Perhaps it's only indigestion.

HAWTREE. Then you are not dead?

GEORGE. Dead, no. Where's my wife?

HAWTREE. You were reported killed.

GEORGE. It wasn't true.

HAWTREE. Alive! My old friend alive!

GEORGE. And well. [*Shakes hands.*] Landed this morning. Where's my wife?

SAM [*who has popped his head from under tablecloth.*] He ain't dead, Poll—he's alive!   [POLLY *rises from under table slowly.*

POLLY [*pause; approaches him, touches him, retreats*]. George! [*He nods.*] George! George!

GEORGE. Yes! Yes!

POLLY. Alive!—My dear George!—Oh, my dear brother!—[*Looking at him intensely.*]—Alive! [*Going to him.*] Oh, my dear, dear brother!—[*In his arms.*]—how could you go and do so? [*Laughs hysterically.*]   [*Pause.*

GEORGE. Where's Esther?

HAWTREE. Here—in this house.

GEORGE. Here!—doesn't she know I'm back?

POLLY. No; how should she?

GEORGE [*to* HAWTREE]. Didn't you get my telegram?

HAWTREE. No; where from?

GEORGE. Southampton! I sent it to the Club.

HAWTREE. I haven't been there these three days.

POLLY [*hysterically*]. Oh, my dear, dear, dear dead-and-gone!—come back all alive, oh, brother George!

SAM. Glad to see yer, sir.

GEORGE. Thank you, Gerridge. [*Shakes hands.*] Same to you—but Esther?

POLLY [*back to audience, and 'kerchief to her eyes*]. She's asleep in her room.   [GEORGE *is going to door;* POLLY *stops him.*

POLLY. You mustn't see her!

GEORGE. Not see her!—after this long absence?—why not?

HAWTREE. She's ill to-day. She has been greatly excited. The news of your death, which we all mourned, has shaken her terribly.

GEORGE. Poor girl! poor girl!

POLLY. Oh, we all cried so when you died!—[*Crying*]—and now you're alive again, I want to cry ever so much more. [*Crying.*

HAWTREE. We must break the news to her gently and by degrees.
[*Crosses to fire, taking his tea with him.*

SAM. Yes. If you turn the tap on to full pressure, she'll explode!
[SAM *turns to* HAWTREE, *who is just raising cup to his lips, and brings it down on saucer with a bang; both annoyed.*

GEORGE. To return, and not to be able to see her—to love her—to kiss her! [*Stamps.*

POLLY. Hush!

GEORGE. I forgot! I shall wake her!

POLLY. More than that—you'll wake the baby!

GEORGE. Baby!—what baby?

POLLY. Yours.

GEORGE. Mine?—mine?

POLLY. Yes—yours and Esther's! Why, didn't you know there was a baby?

GEORGE. No!

POLLY. La! the ignorance of these men!

HAWTREE. Yes, George, you're a father.

GEORGE. Why wasn't I told of this? Why didn't you write?

POLLY. How could we when you were dead?

SAM. And 'adn't left your address.
[*Looks at* HAWTREE, *who turns away quickly.*

GEORGE. If I can't see Esther, I will see the child. The sight of me won't be too much for its nerves. Where is it?

POLLY. Sleeping in its mother's arms. [GEORGE *goes to door; she intercepts him.*] Please not! Please not!

GEORGE. I must. I will.

POLLY. It might kill her, and you wouldn't like to do that. I'll fetch the baby; but, oh, please don't make a noise! You won't make a noise—you'll be as quiet as you can, won't you? Oh! I can't believe it.   [*Exit* POLLY.

[SAM *dances break-down and finishes up looking at* HAWTREE, *who turns away astonished.* SAM *disconcerted;* GEORGE *at door.*

GEORGE. My baby; my ba— It's a dream! You've seen it. [*To* SAM.] What's it like?

SAM. Oh! it's like a—like a sort of—infant—white and—milky, and all that.

[*Enter* POLLY, *with baby wrapped in shawls.* GEORGE *shuts door and meets her.*

POLLY. Gently, gently—take care! Esther will hardly have it touched.   [SAM *rises and gets near to* GEORGE.

GEORGE. But I'm it's father.

POLLY. That don't matter. She's very particular.

GEORGE. Boy or girl?

POLLY. Guess.

GEORGE. Boy! [POLLY *nods.* GEORGE *proud.*] What's his name?

POLLY. Guess.

GEORGE. George? [POLLY *nods.*] Eustace? [POLLY *nods.*] Fairfax? Algernon? [POLLY *nods; pause.*] My names!

SAM [*to* GEORGE]. You'd 'ardly think there was room enough in 'im to 'old so many names, would yer?

[HAWTREE *looks at him—turns to fire.* SAM *disconcerted again.*

GEORGE. To come back all the way from India to find that I'm dead, and that you're alive. To find my wife a widow with a new love aged—How old are you? I'll buy you a pony to-morrow, my brave little boy? What's his weight? I should say two pound nothing. My—baby—my—boy! [*Bends over him and kisses him.*] Take him away, Polly, for fear I should break him.   [POLLY *takes child, and places it in cradle.*

HAWTREE [*crosses to piano. Passes* SAM *front—stares.* SAM *goes round to fireplace, flings down bread and butter in a rage and drinks his tea out of saucer.*] But tell us how it is you're back— how you escaped.

GEORGE. By and by. Too long a story just now. Tell *me* all about it. [POLLY *gives him chair.*] How is it Esther's living here?

POLLY. She came back after the baby was born and the furniture was sold up.

GEORGE. Sold up? What furniture?

POLLY. That you bought for her.

HAWTREE. It couldn't be helped, George.—Mrs. D'Alroy was so poor.

GEORGE. Poor! but I left her six hundred pounds to put in the bank!

HAWTREE. We *must* tell you. She gave it to her father, who banked it in his own name.

SAM. And lost it in bettin'—every copper.

GEORGE. Then she's been in want?

POLLY. No—not in want. Friends lent her money.

GEORGE. What friends? [*Pause; he looks at* POLLY, *who indicates* HAWTREE.] You?

POLLY. Yes.

GEORGE [*rising, and shaking* HAWTREE'S *hand*]. Thank you, old fella. [HAWTREE *droops his head.*

SAM [*aside*]. Now who'd ha' thought that long swell 'ad it in 'im? 'E never mentioned it.

GEORGE. So Papa Eccles had the money? [*Sitting again.*
SAM. And blued it! [*Sits on left corner of table.*
POLLY [*pleadingly*]. You see, Father was very unlucky on the race-course. He told us that if it hadn't been that all his calculations were upset by a horse winning who had no business to, he should have made our fortunes. Father's been unlucky, and he gets tipsy at times, but he's a very clever man, if you only give him scope enough.

SAM. I'd give 'im scope enough!

GEORGE. Where is he now?

SAM. Public-house.

GEORGE. And how is he?

SAM. Drunk! [POLLY *pushes him off table.* SAM *sits at fireplace.*
GEORGE [*to* HAWTREE]. You were right. There is *something* in caste. [*Aloud.*] But tell us all about it.

POLLY. Well, you know, you went away; and then the baby was born. Oh! he was such a sweet little thing, just like—your eyes—your hair.

GEORGE. Cut that!

POLLY. Well, baby came; and when baby was six days old your letter came, Major [*to* HAWTREE]. I saw that it was from India, and that it wasn't in your hand [*to* GEORGE]; I guessed what was inside it, so I opened it unknown to her, and I read there of your capture and death. I daren't tell her. I went to Father to ask his advice, but he was too tipsy to understand me. Sam fetched the doctor. He told us that the news would kill her. When she woke up she said she had dreamt there was a letter from you. I told her no; and day after day she asked for a letter. So the doctor advised us to write one as if it came from you. So we did. Sam and I and the doctor told her—told Esther, I mean, that her eyes were bad, and she mustn't read, and we read our letter to her; didn't we, Sam? But, bless you! she always knew it hadn't come from you! At last, when she was stronger, we told her all.

GEORGE [*after a pause*]. How did she take it?

POLLY. She pressed the baby in her arms, and turned her face to the wall. [*A pause.*] Well, to make a long story short, when she got up she found that Father had lost all the money you left her. There was a dreadful scene between them. She told him he'd robbed her and her child, and Father left the house, and swore he'd never come back again.

SAM. Don't be alarmed—'e did come back.

POLLY. Oh, yes; he was too good-hearted to stop long from his children. He has his faults, but his good points, when you find 'em, are wonderful!

SAM. Yes, when you find 'em!

[*Rises, gets bread and butter from table, and sits by table.*

POLLY. So she had to come back here to us; and that's all.

GEORGE. Why didn't she write to my mother?

POLLY. Father wanted her; but she was too proud—she said she'd die first.

GEORGE [*rising, to* HAWTREE]. There's a woman! Caste's all humbug. [*Sees sword over mantelpiece.*] That's my sword and a map of India, and that's the piano I bought her—I'll swear to the silk!

POLLY. Yes; that was bought in at the sale.

GEORGE [*to* HAWTREE]. Thank ye, old fella!

HAWTREE. Not by me;—I was in India at the time.

GEORGE. By whom, then?

POLLY. By Sam. [SAM *winks at her to discontinue.*] I shall! He knew Esther was breaking her heart about anyone else having it, so he took the money he'd saved up for our wedding, and we're going to be married now—ain't we, Sam?

SAM [*rushing to* GEORGE *and pulling out circulars from pocket*]. And hope by constant attention to business to merit—

POLLY. Since you died it hasn't been opened, but if I don't play it to-night, may I die an old maid!

> [GEORGE *crosses to* SAM, *and shakes his hand, then goes up stage, pulls up blind, and looks into street.* SAM *turns up and meets* POLLY *top of table.*

HAWTREE [*aside*]. Now who'd have thought that little cad had it in him? He never mentioned it. [*Aloud.*] *Apropos*, George, your mother—I'll go to the square and tell her of—

GEORGE. Is she in town?

HAWTREE. Yes. Will you come with me?

GEORGE. And leave my wife?—and such a wife!

HAWTREE. I'll go at once. I shall catch her before dinner. Good-bye, old fellow. Seeing you back again, alive and well, makes me feel quite—that I quite feel—[*Shakes* GEORGE'S *hand. Goes to door, then crosses to* SAM, *who has turned* POLLY'S *tea into his saucer, and is just about to drink; seeing* HAWTREE, *he puts it down quickly, and turns his back.*] Mr. Gerridge, I fear I have often made myself very offensive to you.

SAM. Well, sir, yer 'ave!

HAWTREE. I feared so. I didn't know you then. I beg your pardon. Let me ask you to shake hands—to forgive me, and forget it. [*Offering his hand.*

SAM [*taking it*]. Say no more, sir; and if ever I've made myself offensive to you, I ask your pardon; forget it, and forgive me. [*They shake hands warmly; as* HAWTREE *crosses to the door, recovering from* SAM'S *hearty shake of the hand,* SAM *runs to him.*] Hi, sir! When yer marry that young lady as I know you're engaged to, if you should furnish a house, and require anything in my way—

> [*Bringing out circular; begins to read it.* POLLY *pushes* SAM *away.* SAM *goes and sits in low chair by fireplace, disconcerted, cramming circulars into his pocket.*

HAWTREE. Good-bye, George, for the present. [*At door.*] 'Bye, Polly. [*Resumes his Pall Mall manner as he goes out.*] I'm off to the square.　　　　　　　　　　　　　　　　　[*Exit* HAWTREE.

GEORGE [*at cradle*]. But Esther?

POLLY. Oh, I forgot all about Esther. I'll tell her all about it.

GEORGE. How?

POLLY. I don't know; but it will come. Providence will send it to me, as it has sent you, my dear brother. [*Embracing him.*] You don't know how glad I am to see you back again! You must go. [*Pushing him.* GEORGE *takes hat off piano.*] Esther will be getting up directly. [*At door with* GEORGE, *who looks through keyhole.*] It's no use looking there; it's dark.

GEORGE. It isn't often a man can see his own widow.

POLLY. And it isn't often that he wants to! Now you must go.

　　　　　　　　　　　　　　　　　　　　　　[*Pushing him off.*

GEORGE. I shall stop outside.

SAM. And I'll whistle for you when you may come in.

POLLY. Now—hush!

GEORGE [*opening door wide*]. Oh, my Esther, when you know I'm alive! I'll marry you all over again, and we'll have a second honeymoon, my darling.　　　　　　　　　　　　　　　[*Exit.*

POLLY. Oh, Sam! Sam! [*Commences to sing and dance.* SAM *also dances; they meet in centre of stage, join hands, and dance around two or three times, leaving* SAM *left of* POLLY, *near table.*] Oh, Sam, I'm so excited, I don't know what to do. What shall I —what shall I do?

SAM [*taking up* HAWTREE'S *bread and butter*]. 'Ave a bit of bread and butter, Polly.

POLLY. Now, Sam, light the gas; I'm going to wake her up. [*Opening the door.*] Oh, my darling, if I dare tell you! [*Whispering.*] He's come back! He's come back! He's come back! Alive! Alive! Alive! Sam, kiss me!

> [SAM *rushes to* POLLY, *kisses her, and she jumps off,* SAM *shutting the door.*

SAM [*dances shutter dance*]. I'm glad the swells are gone; now I can open my safety-valve, and let my feelin's escape. To think of 'is comin' back alive from India, just as I am goin' to open my shop. Perhaps he'll get me the patronage of the Royal Family. It would look stunnin' over the door, a lion and a unicorn a-standin' on their 'ind-legs, doin' nothing' furiously, with a lozenge between 'em—thus. [*Seizes plate on table, puts his left foot on chair right of table, and imitates the picture of the Royal arms.*] Polly said I was to light up, and whatever Polly says must be done. [*Lights brackets over mantelpiece, then candles; as he lights the broken one, says*]. Why this one is for all the world like old Eccles! [*Places candles on piano, and sits on music-stool.*] Poor Esther! to think of my knowin' 'er when she was in the ballet line—then in the 'onourable line; then a mother—no, *honourables* is 'mammas'—then a widow, and then in the ballet line again!—and 'im to come back (*growing affected*)—and find a baby, with all 'is furniture and fittin's ready for immediate use—and she, poor thing, lyin' asleep, with 'er eye-lids, 'ot and swollen, not knowin' that that great, big, 'eavy, 'ulking, overgrown dragoon is prowlin' outside, ready to fly at 'er lips, and strangle 'er in 'is strong, lovin' arms —it—it—it——

> [*Breaks down and sobs with his head upon the table.*

Enter POLLY

POLLY. Why, Sam! What's the matter?

SAM [*rises*]. I dunno. The water's got into my meter.

POLLY. Hush! here's Esther.

Enter ESTHER. *They stop suddenly.*

SAM [*singing and dancing*]. 'Tiddy-ti-tum', &c.

ESTHER [*sitting near fire, taking up costume and beginning to work*]. Sam, you seem in high spirits to-night?

SAM. Yes; yer see Polly and I are goin' to be married—and—and —'opes by bestowing a merit—to continue the favour—

POLLY [*who has kissed* ESTHER *two or three times*]. What are you talking about?

SAM. I don't know—I'm off my burner.

[POLLY *goes round to chair and sits facing* ESTHER.

ESTHER. What's the matter with you tonight, dear? I can see something in your eyes.

SAM. P'r'aps it's the new furniture!   [*Sits on music-stool.*

ESTHER. Will you help me with the dress, Polly?

POLLY. It was a pretty dress when it was new—not unlike the one Mademoiselle Delphine used to wear. [*Suddenly clapping her hands.*] Oh!

ESTHER. What's the matter?

POLLY. A needle! [*Crosses to* SAM, *who examines finger.*] I've got it!

SAM. What—the needle—in your finger?

POLLY. No; an idea in my head!

SAM [*still looking at finger*]. Does it 'urt?

POLLY. Stupid! Do you recollect Mademoiselle Delphine, Esther?

ESTHER. Yes.

POLLY. Do you recollect her in that ballet that old Herr Griffen-haagen arranged?—*Jeanne la Folle; or The Return of the Soldier*?

ESTHER. Yes; will you do the fresh hem?

POLLY. What's the use? Let me see—how did it go? How well I remember the scene!—the cottage was on that side, the bridge at the back—then ballet of villagers, and the entrance of Delphine as Jeanne, the bride—tra-lal-lala-lala-la-la. [*Sings and pantomimes,* SAM *imitating her.*] The entrance of Claude, the bridegroom—[*to* SAM, *imitating swell*] How-de-do? How-de-do?

SAM [*rising*]. 'Ow are yer? [*Imitating* POLLY, *then sitting again.*

POLLY. Then there was the procession to church—the march of the soldiers over the bridge—[*sings and pantomimes*]—arrest of Claude, who is drawn for the conscription [ESTHER *looks dreamily*], and is torn from the arms of his bride at the church porch. *Omnes* broken-hearted. This is *Omnes* broken-hearted.
[*Pantomimes.*

ESTHER. Polly, I don't like this; it brings back memories.

POLLY [*going to table, and leaning her hands on it, looks at* ESTHER]. Oh, fuss about memories!—one can't mourn for ever. [ESTHER *surprised.*] Everything in this world isn't sad. There's bad news, and—there's good news sometimes—when we least expect it.

ESTHER. Ah! not for me.

POLLY. Why not?

ESTHER [*anxiously*]. Polly!

POLLY. Second Act! [*This is to be said quickly, startling* SAM, *who has been looking on the ground during the last four or five lines.*] Winter—the Village Pump. This is the village pump [*pointing to* SAM, *seated by piano, on music-stool.* SAM *turns round on music-stool, disgusted.*] Entrance of Jeanne—now called Jeanne la Folle, because she has gone mad on account of the supposed loss of her husband.

SAM. The supposed loss?

POLLY. The supposed loss!

ESTHER [*dropping costume*]. Polly!

SAM. Mind! [*Aside to* POLLY.

POLLY. Can't stop now! Entrance of Claude, *who isn't dead*, in a captain's uniform—a cloak thrown over his shoulders.

ESTHER. Not dead?

POLLY. Don't you remember the ballet? Jeanne is mad, and can't recognize her husband; and don't, till he shows her the ribbon she gave him when they were betrothed! A bit of ribbon! Sam, have you got a bit of ribbon? Oh, that crape sword-knot, that will do! [*Sam astonished.*

ESTHER. Touch that! [*Rising.*

POLLY. Why not?—it's no use *now!*

ESTHER [*slowly, looking into* POLLY'S *eyes*]. You have heard of George—I know you have—I see it in your eyes. You may tell me—I can bear it—I can indeed—indeed I can. Tell me—he is not dead?   [*Violently agitated.*

POLLY. No!

ESTHER. No?

POLLY. No!

ESTHER [*whispers*]. Thank heaven! You've seen him—I see you have!—I know it!—I feel it! I had a bright dream—I saw him as I slept! Oh, let me know if he is near! Give me some sign —some sound—[POLLY *opens piano*]—some token of his life and presence!

>   [SAM *touches* POLLY *on the shoulder, takes hat, and exit.*
>   POLLY *sits immediately at piano and plays air softly—the same air played by* ESTHER, *Act II, on the treble only.*

ESTHER [*in an ecstasy*]. Oh, my husband! come to me! for I know that you are near! Let me feel your arms clasp round me!— Do not fear for me!—I can bear the sight of you!—[*Door opens, showing* SAM *keeping* GEORGE *back.*]—it will not kill me!—George —love—husband—come, oh, come to me!

>   [GEORGE *breaks away from* SAM, *and coming down behind* ESTHER *places his hands over her eyes; she gives a faint scream, and, turning, falls in his arms.* POLLY *plays the bass as well as treble of the air, forte, then fortissimo. She then plays at random, endeavouring to hide her tears. At last strikes piano wildly, and goes off into a fit of hysterical laughter, to the alarm of* SAM, *who, rushing down as* POLLY *cries* 'Sam! Sam!' *falls on his knees in front of her. They embrace,* POLLY *pushing him contemptuously away afterwards.* GEORGE *sits, and* ESTHER *kneels at his feet—he snatches off* ESTHER'S *cap, and throws it up stage.* POLLY *goes left of* GEORGE, SAM *brings music-stool, and she sits.*

ESTHER. To see you here again—to feel your warm breath upon my cheek—is it real, or am I dreaming?

SAM [*rubbing his head*]. No; it's real.

ESTHER [*embracing* GEORGE]. My darling!

SAM. My darling! [POLLY *on music-stool, which* SAM *has placed for her.* SAM, *kneeling by her, imitates* ESTHER—POLLY *scornfully pushes him away.*] But tell us—tell us how you escaped.

GEORGE. It's a long story; but I'll condense it. I was riding out, and suddenly found myself surrounded and taken prisoner. One of the troop that took me was a fella who had been my servant, and to whom I had done some little kindness. He helped me to escape, and hid me in a sort of cave, and for a long time used to bring me food. Unfortunately, he was ordered away; so he brought another Sepoy to look after me. I felt from the first this man meant to betray me, and I watched him like a lynx during the one day he was with me. As evening drew on, a Sepoy picket was passing. I could tell by the look in the fella's eyes he meant to call out as soon as they were near enough; so I seized him by the throat, and shook the life out of him.

ESTHER. You strangled him?

GEORGE. Yes.

ESTHER. Killed him—dead?

GEORGE. He didn't get up again.

POLLY [*to* SAM]. You never go and kill Sepoys.

[*Pushes him over.*

SAM. No! I pay rates and taxes.

GEORGE. The day after, Havelock and his Scotchmen marched through the village, and I turned out to meet them. I was too done up to join, so I was sent straight on to Calcutta. I got leave, took a berth on the P. and O. boat; the passage restored me. I landed this morning, came on here, and brought in the milk.

Enter the MARQUISE; *she rushes to embrace* GEORGE. *All rise.*

MARQUISE. My dear boy!—my dear, dear boy!

POLLY. Why, see, she's crying! She's glad to see him alive, and back again.

SAM [*profoundly*]. Well! There's always some good in women, even when they're ladies.

MARQUISE [*crossing to* ESTHER]. My dear daughter, we must forget our little differences. [*Kissing her.*] Won't you? How history repeats itself! You will find a similar and as unexpected a return mentioned by Froissart in the chapter that treats of Philip Dartnell——

GEORGE. Yes, Mother—I remember.   [*Kisses her.*

MARQUISE [*to* GEORGE, *aside*]. We must take her abroad, and make a lady of her.

GEORGE. Can't, Mamma—she's ready-made. Nature has done it to our hands.

MARQUISE [*aside, to* GEORGE]. But I won't have the man who smells of putty [SAM *at back. He is listening, and at the word 'putty' throws his cap irritably on table.* POLLY *pacifies him, and makes him sit down beside her on window*], nor the man who smells of beer.

> [*Goes to* ESTHER, *who offers her chair, and sits in chair opposite to her.*

Enter HAWTREE, *pale.*

HAWTREE. George! Oh, the Marchioness is here.

GEORGE. What's the matter?

HAWTREE. Oh, nothing. Yes, there is. I don't mind telling you. I've been thrown. I called at my chambers as I came along and found this.   [*Gives* GEORGE *a note; sits on music-stool.*

GEORGE. From the Countess, Lady Florence's mother. [*Reads.*] 'Dear Major Hawtree,—I hasten to inform you that my daughter Florence is about to enter into an alliance with Lord Saxeby, the eldest son of the Marquis of Loamshire. Under these circumstances, should you think fit to call here again, I feel assured—' Well, perhaps it's for the best. [*Returning letter.*] Caste! you know. Caste! And a marquis is a bigger swell than a major.

HAWTREE. Yes, best to marry in your own rank of life.

GEORGE. If you can find *the* girl. But if ever you find *the* girl, marry her. As to her station——

> 'True hearts are more than coronets,
> And simple faith than Norman blood.'

HAWTREE. Ya-as. But a gentleman should hardly ally himself to a nobody.

GEORGE. My dear fella, Nobody's a mistake—he don't exist. Nobody's nobody! Everybody's somebody.

HAWTREE. Yes. But still—Caste.

GEORGE. Oh, Caste's all right. Caste is a good thing if it's not carried too far. It shuts the door on the pretentious and the vulgar; but it should open the door very wide for exceptional merit. Let brains break through its barriers, and what brains can break through love may leap over.

HAWTREE. Yes. Why George, you're quite inspired—quite an orator. What makes you so brilliant? Your captivity? The voyage? What, then?

GEORGE. I'm in love with my wife!

Enter ECCLES, *drunk, with a bottle of gin in his hand.*

ECCLES [*crossing to centre*]. Bless this 'appy company. May we 'ave in our arms what we love in our 'earts [*goes to head of table*]. Polly, fetch wine-glasses—a tumbler will do for me. Let us drink a toast. Mr. Chairman [*to Marquise*], ladies, and gentlemen—I beg to propose the 'elth of our newly returned warrior, *my son-in-law.* [MARQUISE *shivers.*] The Right Honourable George De Alroy. Get glasses, Polly, and send for a bottle of sherry wine for my ladyship. *My* ladyship! My ladyship! M'lad'ship. [*She half turns to him.*] You and me'll have a dram together on the quiet. So delighted to see you under these altered circum-circum-circum-stangate.

[POLLY, *who has shaken her head at him to desist, in vain, very distressed.*

SAM. Shove 'is 'ead in a bucket!   [*Exit, in disgust.*

HAWTREE [*aside to* GEORGE]. I think I can abate this nuisance—at least, I can remove it.

[*Rises and crosses to* ECCLES, *who has got round to right side of table, leaning on it. He taps* ECCLES *with his stick, first on right shoulder, then on left, and finally sharply on right.* ECCLES *turns round and falls on point of stick—*HAWTREE

I

> *steadying him.* GEORGE *crosses behind, to* MARQUISE, *who has gone to cradle—puts his arm round* ESTHER *and takes her to mantel-piece.*

HAWTREE. Mr. Eccles, don't you think that, with your talent for liquor, if you had an allowance of about two pounds a week, and went to Jersey, where spirits are cheap, that you could drink yourself to death in a year?

ECCLES. I think I could—I'm sure I'll try.

> [*Goes up left of table, steadying himself by it, and sits in chair by fire, with the bottle of gin.* HAWTREE *standing by fire.* ESTHER *and* POLLY *stand embracing, centre. As they turn away from each other—*

GEORGE [*coming across with* ESTHER]. Come and play me that air that used to ring in my ears as I lay awake, night after night, captive in the cave—you know.

> [*He hands* ESTHER *to piano. She plays the air.*

MARQUISE [*bending over the cradle, at end*]. My grandson!

> [ECCLES *falls off the chair in the last stage of drunkenness, bottle in hand.* HAWTREE, *leaning one foot on chair from which* ECCLES *has fallen, looks at him through eyeglass.* SAM *enters, and goes to* POLLY, *behind cradle, and producing wedding-ring from several papers, holds it up before her eyes.* ESTHER *plays until curtain drops.*

POINTS FOR DISCUSSION

1. What is meant by *realism* in dialogue?

2. Find examples from this play of dialogue which seems natural, and other examples which still belong to the older, artificial plays.

3. What is the matter with the plot of this play, when it is considered by modern standards?

4. What is the origin of the term 'Deus ex machina'?

5. Why does the dramatist make George bring in the milk can?

6. The episode of George's reappearance to Polly, Sam, and Hawtree has been so arranged that it causes far less excitement than we might reasonably expect. Why was this necessary?

7. Polly's acting of *Jeanne la Folle* is supposed to be a means of preparing

Esther for the shock of discovering that her husband has returned from the grave. What function has it for the audience?

8. What is meant by 'sentimentality' in drama? What means are used to prevent the emotional passages of the play from becoming sentimental?

9. Has this play a moral? What is the author's attitude towards his subject?

CHAPTER VI

THE MODERN STAGE I

THE GROWTH OF NATURALISM

THE past is always easier to survey than the present. New plays are being produced every week, and it is difficult to know which of these plays will prove significant in the future development of drama. The fact of outstanding importance is that no period since the Elizabethan Age has been richer in dramatic production than the first thirty years of the twentieth century.

So many modern dramas have followed the lead which was given by Robertson, and have striven to attain what has come to be called *naturalism* on the stage, that it is necessary to consider what is meant by this term when it is used of presentations in the theatre. No play, no matter how natural it may appear on the stage, does in fact present life as it really is. The characters in a play speak with far more brilliance, and events happen with far greater rapidity and perfection than those of actuality. But it is possible for the dramatist to create an illusion that what is going on in his play might well be happening in real life if he takes care to make his characters do and say nothing which is in obvious contrast to common experience. In aiming at this 'naturalism', modern dramatists have differed much from the dramatists of the Elizabethan Age, who desired to lift their audience out of themselves by appealing to their imagination, so that they became for the moment part of a world where words and thoughts had a force and intensity infinitely greater than is possible in everyday experience. The audiences of the nineteenth and twentieth centuries have lost the Elizabethan

THE PRINCE'S THEATRE, MANCHESTER, 1869

(A typical picture-frame stage)

capacity for being absorbed into a play. The progress of civilization has made people more self-conscious; and the *picture-frame* stage, as it is called, with its clear line between the actors and the audience, discourages the contact between the players and the watchers which was inevitable in the Elizabethan theatre. The contact between actors and audience in a modern theatre is more subtle. It is a kind of delicate sympathy which demands that the actors shall behave as though they are members of the audience; in the Elizabethan theatre, it was the audience who behaved, in imagination, as though they were themselves the actors.

It was the Norwegian dramatist Henrik Ibsen who first showed what powerful effects can be produced when a play creates an illusion in the audience that they are watching an episode in life as they know it in the world outside the theatre. Just as the Restoration dramatists had made their plays a magnifying glass through which to examine the manners of the seventeenth century so Ibsen gave his audiences a critical insight into some of the morals of the nineteenth. As he wrote in one of his letters: 'Everything that I have written has the closest possible connection with what I have lived through, even though it has not been my own experience.' In such plays as *Ghosts* and *A Doll's House* Ibsen showed how easy it is for men to hide reality from themselves behind a veil of false romanticism, a critical attitude summed up in the title of a third play, *The Pretenders*.

The dramatic situations that Ibsen chooses have an affinity with those of Greek Drama. In the words of W. H. Hudson: 'The roots of his actions often run far down into the past; but when the curtain rises on the first scene we have already reached the beginning of the end, and the stage presentation is concerned only with the last term of a long series of events.' When we see him in *A Doll's House* Torvald Helmer

is already the father of three children and has built up over
the years an image of himself as the strong successful husband
protecting his charming but rather childlike wife Norah from
all harm and danger. As the play opens this false image is
about to be destroyed. In *Ghosts*, the man responsible for its
events is already dead before the actors appear on the stage.
Captain Alving lived and died in public esteem before a curtain of respectability kept in position by his wife. In the play
this curtain is drawn back to show the truth and its appalling
consequences.

In their theatrical presentation Ibsen's plays are models of
dramatic structure and had a profound influence on English
dramatists through the translations of William Archer and
the writings of George Bernard Shaw. Their weakness is that
the defects of society change from one generation to another
and the very effectiveness of Ibsen in exposing part of the
hypocrisy of his day made some of his plays the instrument
of their own obsolescence. The protest of Norah Helmer as
she bangs the door behind her at the end of *A Doll's House* is
against a status of women which no longer exists. The reti-
cence of Mrs. Alving and Pastor Manders is hardly a characteristic of the twentieth century, when the sexual escapades
of public figures are given too much rather than too little
publicity. In this book an extract has been chosen from *An
Enemy of the People* because it examines a conflict between
an individual and the society to which he belongs. Conflicts
of this kind are likely to recur, whatever changes there
may be in the structure of the society within which they
develop.

Dr. Thomas Stockmann, who becomes 'an enemy of the
people', is what we should call the Medical Officer of Health
of a coast town in southern Norway of which his brother,
Peter Stockmann, is the Mayor. To attract holiday-makers

some municipal baths have been built, of which the town is very proud. Shortly after the play begins Dr. Stockmann receives the results of an analysis of the water supply of the baths confirming his suspicions that it is so badly contaminated with sewage that, instead of contributing to the health of those using them, the baths are a source of disease. Dr. Stockmann is naïve enough to suppose that there will be a widespread welcome for his discovery but he quickly comes into conflict with his brother, the Mayor, who is only too well aware of all the vested interests in the town that will suffer if the bacteriological report is published. He refuses to bring the Report before the Board responsible for the baths, so Dr. Stockmann sends it for publication to the local paper, the *People's Herald*, of which Hovstad is the editor and Aslaksen the printer. The extract begins when they are about to publish what Dr. Stockmann has sent.

AN ENEMY OF THE PEOPLE

by HENRIK IBSEN

Translated by JAMES WALTER MCFARLANE

ASLAKSEN. I say, Mr. Hovstad!

HOVSTAD. Well, well—what is it?

ASLAKSEN. The Mayor's out there in the printing shop.

HOVSTAD. The Mayor, did you say?

ASLAKSEN. Yes, he wants a word with you. He came in the back way—didn't want to be seen, I suppose.

HOVSTAD. What does he want, I wonder? No, wait here, I'll go myself——

[*He goes over to the door into the printing shop, opens it and invites the* MAYOR *in.*

HOVSTAD. Aslaksen, keep an eye open to see that nobody——

ASLAKSEN. I understand.

[*He goes into the printing shop.*

MAYOR. I don't suppose you were expecting me here, Mr. Hovstad.

HOVSTAD. No, as a matter of fact I wasn't.

MAYOR [*looking about him*]. You've settled yourself in here nice and comfortably. Very nice.

HOVSTAD. Oh——

MAYOR. And here I come without any appointment, and proceed to take up all your precious time.

HOVSTAD. *Please*, Mr. Mayor, I'm only too delighted to be of service. Let me take your things. [*He puts the* MAYOR'S *hat and stick on a chair*.] Now, won't you sit down?

MAYOR [*sits at the table*]. Thank you.

[HOVSTAD *also sits down at the table*.

MAYOR. I have had an extremely disagreeable matter to deal with today, Mr. Hovstad.

HOVSTAD. Really? Of course, with so many things to see to——

MAYOR. This particular matter has been raised by the Medical Officer of the Baths.

HOVSTAD. By the Doctor?

MAYOR. He's written a kind of report about a number of alleged shortcomings at the Baths, and sent it to the Board.

HOVSTAD. Has he?

MAYOR. Yes, hasn't he told you? I thought he said——

HOVSTAD. Oh yes, that's right! He did mention something about——

ASLAKSEN [*coming from the printing shop*]. I'd better have that manuscript——

HOVSTAD [*angrily*]. It's on the desk there.

ASLAKSEN [*finds it*]. Good.

MAYOR. But I say, surely *that's*——

ASLAKSEN. Yes, that's the Doctor's article, Mr. Mayor.

HOVSTAD. Oh, is *that* what you were talking about?

MAYOR. Precisely. What do you think of it?

HOVSTAD. I'm no expert, of course, and I've only just glanced at it.

MAYOR. Yet you are printing it?

HOVSTAD. I can't very well refuse a man in his position——

ASLAKSEN. I've got no say in what goes into the paper, Mr. Mayor——

MAYOR. Of course not.

ASKLAKSEN. I just print what I'm given.

MAYOR. Quite so.

ASLAKSEN. So if you'll excuse me——

[*He walks across towards the printing shop.*

MAYOR. Just a moment, please, Mr. Aslaksen. With your permission, Mr. Hovstad——

HOVSTAD. Please.

MAYOR. Now you are a wise and sensible sort of man, Mr. Aslaksen.

ASLAKSEN. I am very pleased you should think so, Mr. Mayor.

MAYOR. And a man of considerable influence in some circles.

ASLAKSEN. Mainly among the people of moderate means.

MAYOR. The small ratepayers are in the majority—here as everywhere else.

ASLAKSEN. That's right.

MAYOR. And I've no doubt you know what most of them think about things in general. Isn't that so?

ASLAKSEN. Yes, I think I can safely say I do, Mr. Mayor.

MAYOR. Well—the fact that this admirable spirit of self-sacrifice is to be found in our town among its less well-endowed citizens——

ASLAKSEN. How do you mean?

HOVSTAD. Self-sacrifice?

MAYOR. —This shows an admirable public spirit, most admirable. I almost said unexpected, too. But of course you know better than I what people's attitudes are.

ASLAKSEN. But, Mr. Mayor——

MAYOR. And in fact it's no small sacrifice that the town will have to make.

HOVSTAD. The town?

ASLAKSEN. But I don't understand—You mean the Baths, surely——

MAYOR. At a rough estimate, the alterations which the Medical

Officer considers desirable will come to something like a couple of hundred thousand crowns.

ASLAKSEN. That's a lot of money, but——

MAYOR. Of course it will be necessary to raise a municipal loan.

HOVSTAD [rises]. Surely it's not the idea that the town——?

ASLAKSEN. It's not going to come out of the rates! Not out of the people's pockets!

MAYOR. My dear Mr. Aslaksen, where else do you see the money coming from?

ASLAKSEN. I think the owners ought to take care of that.

MAYOR. The owners do not see themselves in a position to provide any additional capital.

ASLAKSEN. Is that absolutely certain, Mr. Mayor?

MAYOR. I am assured on that point. If all these extensive alterations are considered desirable, the town itself must pay for them.

ASLAKSEN. But God damn it all—I beg your pardon!—but this puts a completely different light on things, Mr. Hovstad!

HOVSTAD Yes, it does indeed.

MAYOR. The most ruinous thing is that we'll be forced to close the Baths for a couple of years.

HOVSTAD. Close them? Completely?

ASLAKSEN. For two years?

MAYOR. Yes, the work will take all that long—at least.

ASLAKSEN. Yes, but Heavens! We could never last out that long, Mr. Mayor. What would people like us live on in the meantime?

MAYOR. I regret to say that is an extremely difficult question to answer, Mr. Aslaksen. But what do you expect us to do? Do you think anybody is going to come here if you get people going round making up these stories about the water being polluted, and about the place being a cesspool, and the whole town——

ASLAKSEN. Do you think the whole thing might just be imagination?

MAYOR. With the best will in the world, I cannot come to any other conclusion.

ASLAKSEN. Then I must say Dr. Stockmann is being most irresponsible in all this. You must forgive me, Mr. Mayor, but——

MAYOR. I regret what you say is quite true, Mr. Aslaksen. My brother has always been rather impetuous, unfortunately.

ASLAKSEN. Are you still prepared to support him after this, Mr. Hovstad?

HOVSTAD. But who would have thought——?

MAYOR. I have drawn up a short statement of the facts, putting a rather more sober interpretation on them; and in it I have suggested some ways in which such defects as may come to light could reasonably be dealt with without going beyond the present resources of the Baths.

HOVSTAD. Have you this statement with you, Mr. Mayor?

MAYOR [*fumbling in his pocket*]. Yes, I brought it with me on the off-chance that——

ASLAKSEN [*hastily*]. Heavens above, there he is!

MAYOR. Who? My brother?

HOVSTAD. Where?

ASLAKSEN. He's coming in through the printing shop.

MAYOR. It *would* happen. I don't want to bump into him here, and there was still a lot more I wanted to talk to you about.

HOVSTAD [*points to the door on the right*]. In there for the present.

MAYOR. But——!

HOVSTAD. There's only Billing in there.

ASLAKSEN. Quick, quick! He's coming now.

MAYOR. All right. But see if you can't get rid of him quickly.

[*He goes out through the door, right, which* ASLAKSEN *opens, and shuts again behind him.*

HOVSTAD. Pretend you are doing something, Aslaksen.

[*He sits down and begins to write.* ASLAKSEN *rummages through a pile of newspapers on a chair, right.*

DR. STOCKMANN [*entering from the printing shop*]. Back again!

[*He puts down his hat and stick.*

HOVSTAD [*writing*]. Already, Doctor? Hurry up with what we were talking about, Aslaksen. We haven't got a lot of time to spare today.

DR. STOCKMANN. No proofs yet, they tell me.

ASLAKSEN [*without turning round*]. You could hardly expect them yet, Doctor.

DR. STOCKMANN. Well, well, it's just that I'm impatient—as you can well imagine. I can't settle to anything until I've seen the thing in print.

HOVSTAD. Hm! It'll be a good while yet, I fancy. Don't you think so, Aslaksen?

ASLAKSEN. Yes, I'm rather afraid so.

DR. STOCKMANN. Never mind, my dear fellows. I'll look in again. I don't mind coming twice if need be. An important thing like this—the welfare of the whole town—this is no time for dawdling on. [*About to go, but stops and comes back.*] Actually—there was something else I wanted to talk to you about.

HOVSTAD. Excuse me, but couldn't we perhaps make it some other time——?

DR. STOCKMANN. It won't take a second. You see it's just that—when people read my article in the paper tomorrow morning, and realize that all through the winter I have been quietly working away in the interests of the town——

HOVSTAD. Yes, but Doctor——

DR. STOCKMANN. I know what you are going to say. You think I was only damn' well doing my duty—my simple duty as a citizen. Of course! I know that as well as you do. But my fellow citizens, you know—Well, I mean, they think rather highly of me, actually, these good people——

ASLAKSEN. Yes, the people have thought very highly of you up to now, Dr. Stockmann.

DR. STOCKMANN. Yes, and that's just what I'm a little bit afraid of—What I mean is—a thing like this comes along, and they—especially the underprivileged classes—take it as a rousing call to take the affairs of the town into their own hands in future.

HOVSTAD [*rising*]. Hm! Dr. Stockmann, I don't think I ought to conceal from you——

DR. STOCKMANN. Aha! I might have guessed there'd be something in the wind. But I won't hear of it! If anybody's thinking of organizing anything like that——

HOVSTAD. Like what?

DR. STOCKMANN. Well, anything at all—a parade or a banquet or a presentation—whatever it is, you must promise me faithfully to put a stop to it. And you too, Mr. Aslaksen! I insist!

HOVSTAD. Excuse me, Doctor, but sooner or later you've got to hear the real truth——

[MRS. STOCKMANN, *in hat and coat, enters by the main door, back, left.*

MRS. STOCKMANN [*sees the* DOCTOR]. Just as I thought!

HOVSTAD [*goes over to her*]. You here too, Mrs. Stockmann?

DR. STOCKMANN. What the devil do you want here, Katherine?

MRS. STOCKMANN. You know very well what I want.

HOVSTAD. Won't you take a seat? Or perhaps——

MRS. STOCKMANN. Thanks, but don't you bother about me. And you must forgive me coming here to fetch my husband; for I'm the mother of three children, I'll have you know.

DR. STOCKMANN. What's all this rubbish! We all know that!

MRS. STOCKMANN. But it doesn't look as if you care very much these days about your wife and children; otherwise you wouldn't be carrying on as you are, bringing us all to rack and ruin.

DR. STOCKMANN. Have you gone stark, staring mad, Katherine? Are you trying to say a man with wife and children has no right to proclaim the truth—has no right to be a useful and active citizen—has no right to be of service to the town he lives in?

MRS. STOCKMANN. Do be reasonable, Thomas!

ASLAKSEN. Just what I say. Moderation in all things.

MRS. STOCKMANN. That's why it's very wrong of you, Mr. Hovstad, to lure my husband away from house and home and fool him into getting mixed up in all this.

HOVSTAD. I don't go about fooling people——

DR. STOCKMANN. Fool me! Do you think I'd let anybody make a fool of *me*!

MRS. STOCKMANN. Yes, you would. I know, I know, you are the cleverest man in town. But you're too easily fooled, Thomas. [*To* HOVSTAD.] Remember, if you print what he's written he loses his job at the Baths——

ASLAKSEN. What!

HOVSTAD. You know, Doctor——

DR. STOCKMANN [*laughs*]. Ha ha! Just let them try! Oh no, they wouldn't dare. You see, I have the compact majority behind me.

MRS. STOCKMANN. Yes, worse luck! Fancy having a nasty thing like that behind you.

DR. STOCKMANN. Fiddlesticks, Katherine! Go home and look to your house and let me look to society. Why should you be so afraid; I'm quite confident, and really rather pleased with things. [*Walks up and down, rubbing his hands.*] Truth and the People will prevail, you can take your oath on that. Oh, I see the massed ranks of a great citizen army marching on to victory—! [*Stops by a chair.*] What the devil is *that*?

ASLAKSEN [*turns to look*]. Oh!

HOVSTAD [*similarly*]. Hm!

DR. STOCKMANN. There lies the highest mark of authority.

[*He picks the* MAYOR'S *hat up carefully by the tips of his fingers and holds it aloft.*

MRS. STOCKMANN. The Mayor's hat!

DR. STOCKMANN. And here the baton of office, too. How in the name of glory——?

HOVSTAD. Well——

DR. STOCKMANN. Ah, I see! He's been here trying to talk you over. Ha ha! Came to the right man, eh? Then he must have seen me in the printing shop. [*Bursts into laughter.*] Did he run away, Mr. Aslaksen?

ASLAKSEN [*hurriedly*]. Yes, Doctor, he ran away.

DR. STOCKMANN. Ran away without either his stick or—Rubbish, Peter never runs away from anything. But what the devil have you done with him? Ah—in there, of course. Now I'll show you something, Katherine!

MRS. STOCKMANN. Thomas—please!

ASLAKSEN. Have a care, Doctor!

[DR. STOCKMANN *puts the* MAYOR'S *hat on, takes his stick, walks over and throws open the door, and stands there saluting. The* MAYOR *comes in, red with anger; behind him comes* BILLING.

MAYOR. What's the meaning of all this tomfoolery?

DR. STOCKMANN. Show some respect, my dear Peter. I'm the one in authority here now. [*He walks up and down.*

MRS. STOCKMANN [*near to tears*]. Oh, Thomas, really!

MAYOR [*following him about*]. Give me my hat and my stick!

DR. STOCKMANN [*as before*]. You might be chief constable, but I am the Mayor—I'm head of the whole town, can't you see!

MAYOR. Take that hat off, I tell you. Don't forget it's an official badge of office.

DR. STOCKMANN. Pooh! When a people rises from its slumber like a giant refreshed, do you think anybody's going to be scared by a hat? Because you might as well know, we are having a revolution in town tomorrow. You threatened to dismiss me; well now I'm dismissing you, relieving you of all your official positions—Perhaps you think I can't? Oh yes, I can. Because I can bring irresistible social pressure to bear. Hovstad and Billing will put down a barrage in the *People's Herald*, and Aslaksen will sally forth at the head of the entire Ratepayers Association——

ASLAKSEN. Not me, Doctor.

DR. STOCKMANN. Yes of course you will——

MAYOR. Aha! Then perhaps Mr. Hovstad has decided to associate himself with this agitation after all?

HOVSTAD. No, Mr. Mayor.

ASLAKSEN. No, Mr. Hovstad is not so stupid as to go and ruin both the paper and himself for the sake of some wild idea.

DR. STOCKMANN [*looks round*]. What does this mean?

HOVSTAD. You have represented your case in a false light, Dr. Stockmann; consequently I cannot give it my support.

BILLING. And after what the Mayor was kind enough to tell me in there——

DR. STOCKMANN. A false light! You leave that side of things to me. You just print my article—I'm quite ready to stand by everything I say.

HOVSTAD. I'm not going to print it. I cannot and will not and dare not print it.

DR. STOCKMANN. Dare not? What sort of talk is that? You are the editor, aren't you? And it's the editors who control the press, surely?

ASLAKSEN. No, it's the readers.

MAYOR. Fortunately, yes.

ASLAKSEN. It's public opinion, the educated public, the rate-payers and all the others—these are the people who control the press.

DR. STOCKMANN [*calmly*]. And all these forces are against me?

ASLAKSEN. Yes, they are. It would mean total ruin for the town if your article were printed.

DR. STOCKMANN. Indeed.

MAYOR. My hat and my stick!

    [DR. STOCKMANN *takes the hat off and puts it on the table, along with the stick.*

MAYOR [*collecting them both*]. Your term as mayor has come to an abrupt end.

DR. STOCKMANN. This is not the end yet. [*To* HOVSTAD.] So it's quite impossible to get my article in the *Herald*?

HOVSTAD. Quite impossible. And I'm thinking partly also of your family——

MRS. STOCKMANN. Oh, you needn't start worrying about his family, Mr. Hovstad.

MAYOR [*takes a sheet of paper out of his pocket*]. For the guidance of the public, it will be sufficient to print this. It is an official statement.

HOVSTAD [*takes it*]. Good. I'll see that it goes in.

DR. STOCKMANN. But not mine! You think you can gag me and silence the truth! You'll not get away with this so easily. Mr. Aslaksen, will you please take my manuscript and print it for me at once as a pamphlet—at my own expense, and on my authority. I want four hundred copies—no, five—six hundred, I want.

ASLAKSEN. Not if you offered me its weight in gold could I let my printing press be used for a thing like that. I daren't offend public opinion. You'll not get anybody in town to print it, I shouldn't think.

DR. STOCKMANN. Give it back to me then.

HOVSTAD [*hands him the manuscript*]. There you are.

DR. STOCKMANN [*takes his hat and stick*]. I'll get it out somehow. I'll call a mass meeting and read it out! All my fellow citizens shall hear the voice of truth!

MAYOR. You'll never get anybody to hire you a hall.

ASLAKSEN. Absolutely nobody, I'm quite certain.

BILLING. No, I'm damned if they will.

MRS. STOCKMANN. But that would be outrageous! Why is everybody against you all of a sudden?

DR. STOCKMANN [*angrily*]. I'll tell you why. It's because all the men in this town are nothing but a lot of old women—like you. All they can think about is their families; they never think about the rest of the community.

MRS. STOCKMANN [*taking his arm*]. Then I'll show them one—old woman at least who can be a man—for once. I'll stick by you, Thomas!

DR. STOCKMANN. Well said, Katherine. And I *will* have my say, by Heaven! If I can't book a hall, I'll hire a man with a drum to march round town with me, and I'll proclaim it at every street corner.

MAYOR. I can't believe you'd be so absolutely crazy.

DR. STOCKMANN. Oh yes, I would!

ASLAKSEN. You'll not get a single man in the whole of the town to go with you!

BILLING. No, I'm damned if you will!

MRS. STOCKMANN. Don't you give in now, Thomas. I'll get the boys to go with you.

DR. STOCKMANN. That's a wonderful idea!

MRS. STOCKMANN. Morten will love to go; and Ejlif's sure to come along as well.

DR. STOCKMANN. Yes, and then what about Petra! And you too, Katherine?

MRS. STOCKMANN. No, no, not me. But I'll stand in the window and watch, that's what I'll do.

DR. STOCKMANN [*puts his arms round her and kisses her*]. Thank you

K

for that! And now, gentlemen, the gloves are off. We'll see whether you and your shabby tricks can stop an honest citizen who wants to clean up the town.

[*He and his wife go out through the door, back, left.*
MAYOR [*shakes his head thoughtfully*]. Now he's sent her mad, too.

POINTS FOR DISCUSSION

1. What use is made in this scene of dramatic irony?

2. Is there any parallel here with Greek drama other than the use of dramatic irony?

3. What dramatic purpose is served by the incident in which Dr. Stockmann wears his brother's hat and stick?

4. What are the grounds of opposition to Dr. Stockmann?

5. How does the presence of Mrs. Stockmann contribute to the scene?

6. To what extent does Ibsen appear to be on the side of Dr. Stockmann?

7. Why do you think that Ibsen chose to make Dr. Stockmann and the Mayor brothers?

8. What sort of a picture is given of the press? Is it out of date?

9. Discuss the use made in this scene of tension and relaxation and the ways in which they are brought about.

10. Are there any examples of social drama earlier than Ibsen? Can you suggest reasons why it should have developed on any scale towards the end of the nineteenth century?

EXPRESSIONISM

Not all modern drama aims at naturalism. Some of the plays which have been written make no attempt whatever to imitate the occurrences of real life and everyday experience they deliberately exaggerate and distort certain parts of life in order to bring out with startling clearness a new interpretation of ordinary occurrences. These *expressionist* plays resemble the old Moralities in being concerned, not with men but with mankind; not with the behaviour of the individual, but with the behaviour of the masses.

When millions of people are passing their days doing monotonous routine work, and their leisure hours in reading the same newspaper or watching the same film, there is a tendency for them all to think similar thoughts and to lose their identity in a drab sameness of outlook. Such a change comes over people imperceptibly, and they are not themselves aware of their stereotyped attitude to life. It is impossible to show one member of a crowd the futility of what he is doing and thinking by pointing out to him another member of the same crowd, as the second person will be acting and thinking in exactly the same way as the first. In order to appreciate fully what a crowd is doing, you have to be outside the crowd altogether, looking down upon it from some superior station, like one of the gods of old. This is the position of an audience watching an expressionist play. Most dramas have helped a man to get outside himself; expressionist dramas help him to get outside humanity.

These plays are not at all easy to write, as some means has to be found of putting the audience into this position of god-like aloofness. They are not easy to witness, as the audience are unaccustomed to the position of critical detachment which they are expected to maintain all the time, and find it difficult to understand a play which stimulates the intellect but makes no appeal to the sympathetic emotions. A play which solves these difficulties with particular success is that written by two Czechs, the Brothers Čapek, which has been translated into English by Sir Nigel Playfair and Clifford Bax. The official title is 'AND SO *ad infinitum*', but it has come to be called *The Insect Play*.

THE INSECT PLAY

By THE BROTHERS ČAPEK

Translated by NIGEL PLAYFAIR AND CLIFFORD BAX

SCENE: *A sandy hillock—various holes, &c.*

BEETLES *are quarrelling over a* CHRYSALIS, *which is seized first by one then the other.*

CHRYSALIS. The whole world is bursting into blossom. I am being born.

TRAMP [*raising his head—he is lying half asleep*]. How much?

CHRYSALIS. The Great Adventure begins.

TRAMP. Right-ho! [*Settles down again.*]   [*Pause.*

MR. BEETLE [*behind the scenes*]. What yer getting at?

MRS. BEETLE [*behind the scenes*]. Me?

MR. BEETLE. Yes, you—you lump of rubbish.

MRS. BEETLE. Silly swine.

MR. BEETLE. Fathead.

MRS. BEETLE. Fathead yourself—mind where you're going.

[*They enter, rolling a huge ball of dirt*

MR. BEETLE. It's all right, isn't it?

MRS. BEETLE. I'm all of a tremble.

MR. BEETLE. Our capital—that's what it is—our lovely capital—careful—careful.

MRS. BEETLE. Can't be too careful with our capital—our little pile.

MR. BEETLE. How we've saved and scraped and toiled and moiled to come by it.

MRS. BEETLE. Night and morning, toiled and moiled and saved and scraped.

MR. BEETLE. And we've seen it grow and grow, haven't we, bit by bit—our little ball of blessedness.

MRS. BEETLE. Our very own it is.

MR. BEETLE. Our very own.

MRS. BEETLE. Our life's work.

MR. BEETLE. Smell it, old woman—pinch it—feel the weight of it. Ours—ours.

MRS. BEETLE. A godsend.

MR. BEETLE. A blessing—straight from Heaven—capital—capital.

CHRYSALIS. Eternal night is breaking:
The universe is waking:
One minute, just one minute
And I—*I*—shall be in it.

MRS. BEETLE. Husband.

MR. BEETLE. What is it, old woman?

MRS. BEETLE. Ha, ha, ha!

MR. BEETLE. Ha, ha, ha! Wife!

MRS. BEETLE. What is it, old man?

MR. BEETLE. Ha, ha! It's fine to own something—property—the dream of your life, the fruit of your labours.

MRS. BEETLE. Ha, ha, ha!

MR. BEETLE. I'm off my head with joy—I'm going balmy.

MRS. BEETLE. Why?

MR. BEETLE. With worry. Now we've got our little pile that we've so looked forward to, we've got to work and work and work to make another one.

MRS. BEETLE. Why another one?

MR. BEETLE. Silly—so that we can have two, of course.

MRS. BEETLE. Two? Quite right—quite right—two.

MR. BEETLE. Just fancy—two—at least two, say three. Every one who's made his pile has to make another.

MRS. BEETLE. So that he can have two?

MR. BEETLE. Yes, or three.

MRS. BEETLE. Husband.

MR. BEETLE. Well, what is it?

MRS. BEETLE. I'm scared—S'posin' some one was to steal it from us.

MR. BEETLE. What?

MRS. BEETLE. Our capital—our little pile—our all in all.

MR. BEETLE. Our pi-ile—My gawd—don't frighten me.

MRS. BEETLE. We oughtn't to roll it about with us till we've made another one, dearie, did we?

MR. BEETLE. I'll tell you what—we'll invest it—In-vest it—store it up—bury it. That's what we'll do—nice and deep—nice and deep.

MRS. BEETLE. I hope nobody finds it.

MR. BEETLE. Eh, what's that? Finds it—No, of course they won't. Our little bit of capital.

MRS. BEETLE. Our nest-egg—Oh, bless me—I hope no one does —our little all.

MR. BEETLE. Wait—stay here and watch it—Watch it careful— don't let your eyes off it, not for a minute—Capital—Capital.

MRS. BEETLE. Where yer off to?

MR. BEETLE. To look for a hole—a little hole—a deep hole— deep and narrer to bury it in—out of harm's way—Careful— Careful. [*Exit.*

MRS. BEETLE. Husband—husband, come back—wait a bit—I've found one—such a nice hole—Husband! He's gone! If I could only look into it—No, I mustn't leave yer. But only a peep—Here, stay here good and quiet, darling. Hubby'll be back soon—in half a jiff, half a jiff—So long, keep good—half a ji—— [*Enters the lair of the* ICHNEUMON FLY.

CHRYSALIS. Oh, to be born—to be born—into the great new world.

Enter a STRANGE BEETLE

STRANGE BEETLE. They're gone—now's my chance.

[*Rolls pile away.*

TRAMP. 'Ere, mind where yer going to.

STRANGE BEETLE. Mind yer feet.

TRAMP. What's that yer rolling?

STRANGE BEETLE. Ha, ha! That's my capital—my little pile, my all.

TRAMP. Bit niffy, ain't it?

STRANGE BEETLE. Eh?

TRAMP. It smells.

STRANGE BEETLE. Capital don't smell—Off you go, my precious —This way, my little all, my nest-egg, my capital. [*Exit.*

MRS. BEETLE. Oh dear, oh dear. That's somebody's house, that is —We can't put you there, my jewel. Oh, where's it gone to? Where's it gone to? My little pile—where's it gone to?

TRAMP. Why, not 'arf a minute——

MRS. BEETLE [*rushing at him*]. Thief—thief—What 'ave you done with my pile?

TRAMP. I'm telling yer.

MRS. BEETLE. Here, give it back—yer wretch.

TRAMP. Just this minute a gentleman rolled it away over there.

MRS. BEETLE. What gentleman? Who?

TRAMP. A pot-bellied fellow, a fat, round chap.

MRS. BEETLE. My husband?

TRAMP. A feller with an ugly mug and crooked feet.

MRS. BEETLE. That's my husband.

TRAMP. His capital he said it was.

MRS. BEETLE. That's him—he must have found a hole—Husband —My precious—Darling! Where is the blasted fool?

TRAMP. That's where he rolled it to.

MRS. BEETLE. Coo-eh! Couldn't he have called me? Husband, my precious! I'll learn yer—Our capital—our all—our little pile. [*Exit.*

TRAMP. Them butterflies was gay
    And foolish, yer might say:
    But these 'ere beetles—lumme,
    They *do* work, anyway!
    So, 'ere's to wish 'em luck—
    Though gatherin' balls of muck
    Is jest about as rummy
    As anythink I've struck.

CHRYSALIS. O universe, prepare! O space, expand! The mightiest of all happenings is at hand.

TRAMP. What's that?

CHRYSALIS. I'm being born.

TRAMP. That's good—And what are you going to be?

CHRYSALIS. I don't know—I don't know—Something great.

TRAMP. Ah ha!

CHRYSALIS. I'll do something extraordinary—I'm being born.

TRAMP. What *you* want's life, my son.

CHRYSALIS. When half a minute's gone,
      Something immense, unbounded,
    Will happen here.

TRAMP.   Go on!

CHRYSALIS. I shall do something great!

TRAMP. What?

CHRYSALIS. When I change my state,

          The world will be astounded!

TRAMP. Well—'urry up. I'll wait.

[*Enter* ICHNEUMON FLY, *dragging the corpse of a* CRICKET *to its lair*.

ICHNEUMON FLY. Look, Larva, daddy's bringing you something
   nice.   [*Enters his lair*.

CHRYSALIS [*shouting*].

        The torment of my birth

        Is tearing the whole earth.

        She groans to set me free——

TRAMP. Then get a move on. See?

ICHNEUMON FLY [*returning*]. No, no, daughter, you must eat.
  You mustn't come out—it wouldn't do at all. Daddy'll soon
  be back and he'll bring you something nice. What would you
  like, piggywiggy?

              Enter LARVA

LARVA. Daddy, I'm bored here.

ICHNEUMON FLY. Ha, ha! That's a nice thing to say. Give daddy
  a kiss—Daddy'll bring you something tasty. Would you like
  a follow of cricket? Ha, ha—not a bad idea.

LARVA. I'd like—I don't know what I'd like.

ICHNEUMON FLY. She doesn't know what she'd like, bless her little
  heart. I'll find something you'll like—Ta-ta! Daddy must go
  to work now—Daddy must go a hunting and fetch something
  for his popsy-wopsy. Ta-ta! Go back now, poppet, and wait
  for your din-din. Ta-ta!   [*Exit* LARVA.

ICHNEUMON FLY [*to* TRAMP]. Who are you?

TRAMP. I?

ICHNEUMON FLY. Are you edible?

TRAMP. Yes, I don't think.

ICHNEUMON FLY [*sniffing*]. No—not fresh enough—Who are you?

TRAMP. Oh, any sort of skunk, I am.

ICHNEUMON FLY [*bowing*]. Pleased to meet you. Any family?

TRAMP. Not as I am aware of.

ICHNEUMON FLY. Did you see her?

TRAMP. 'Er? Who?

ICHNEUMON FLY. My Larva. Charming, eh? Smart child—And how she grows, and what a twist she's got. Children are a great joy, aren't they?

TRAMP. I've 'eard 'em well spoken of.

ICHNEUMON FLY. Well, of course they are, you take it from me— One who knows. When you have them, at least you know what you're working for. That's life, that is. Children want to grow, to eat, to laugh, to dance, to play, don't they? Am I right?

TRAMP. Children want a lot.

ICHNEUMON FLY. Would you believe it, I take her two or three crickets every day. Do you think she eats them all up? No— Only the titbits—A splendid child, eh?

TRAMP. I should say so.

ICHNEUMON FLY. I'm proud of her—real proud. Takes after me —just like her daddy, eh? Ha, ha! And here I stand gossiping, when I ought to be at work. Oh, the fuss and the running about—Up early, home late, but as long as you're doing it for some one worth doing it for, what does it matter? Am I right?

TRAMP. I suppose you are.

ICHNEUMON FLY. A pity you aren't edible, isn't it? It is, really I must take her something, you know, mustn't I? You see that yourself, don't you?　　　　　[*Fingering* CHRYSALIS.

CHRYSALIS. I proclaim the re-birth of the world.

ICHNEUMON FLY. Ah! You aren't ripe yet—Pity.

CHRYSALIS. I shall inspire—I shall create.

ICHNEUMON FLY. It's a great responsibility to bring up children— A great worry, isn't it? Feeding the poor little mites, paying for their education and putting them out into the world. That's no trifle, I can tell you. Well, I must be off now—Au revoir— Pleased to have met you—Ta-ta, my chicken—Be good! [*Exit*.

TRAMP. This 'as me fairly beat. That fly destroys
　　　The cricket jest to feed 'is girls and boys;

But that pore 'armless cricket found life sweet,
Same as 'e does.—No! Nature 'as me beat!

LARVA [*crawling out of hole*]. Daddy! Daddy!

TRAMP. So you're the Larva. Let's have a look at you.

LARVA. How ugly you are!

TRAMP. Am I? Why?

LARVA. I don't know—oh, how bored I am! I want—I want—

TRAMP. What yer want?

LARVA. I don't know. Yes I do—To tear up something—Something alive—that wriggles.

TRAMP. 'Ere, what's come over yer?

LARVA. Ugly—ugly—ugly!   [*Crawls away.*

TRAMP. Where's Mr. Manners?—Blowed if I'd feed a daughter
Like 'er. Perliteness—that's what *I'd* 'ave taught 'er.

Enter MR. BEETLE

MR. BEETLE [*calling*]. Come along, old girl. I've found a hole.
Where are you? Where's my pile? Where's my wife?

TRAMP. Your wife? Do you mean that old harridan? That greasy
fat bundle of rags?

MR. BEETLE. That's her—Where's my pile?

TRAMP. That old tub in petticoats?

MR. BEETLE. That's her—that's her— She had my pile—What's
she done with my pile?

TRAMP. Why, your beauty went to look for you.

MR. BEETLE. Did she? Where's my pile?

TRAMP. That great ball of muck?

MR. BEETLE. Yes, yes. My nest-egg—my savings—my capital.
Where's my beautiful pile? I left my wife with it.

TRAMP. Some gentleman rolled it away over there. Your wife
wasn't here at the time.

MR. BEETLE. Where was she? Where is she?

TRAMP. She went after him. She thought it was you. She kept
shouting for yer.

MR. BEETLE. I'm not asking about her. Where's my pile, I say?

TRAMP. Gentleman rolled it away.

MR. BEETLE. Rolled it away? My pile? Gawd in 'eaven! Catch him. Catch him. Thief! Murder! All my little lot. All I've saved. They've killed me, they've done me in. Who cares about my wife? It's my pile they've taken. Help—stop thief! Murder!

TRAMP. Ha, ha, ha!

> Crikee! 'E don't want pleasure
> But jest to pile up treasure;
> And when the old sly copper—
> Death—come and nabs 'im proper,
> 'E'll still be a nigger
> Sweatin' to make it bigger,
> Still 'eavin' and still puffin' . . .
> And what's he gained? Why, nuffin'!

MR. CRICKET [*off stage*]. Look out, darling—take care you don't stumble. Here we are—here we are. Oopsidaisy! This is where we live—this is our new little home. Careful—You haven't hurt yourself, have you?

Enter MR. *and* MRS. CRICKET

MRS. CRICKET. No, Cricket, don't be absurd.

MR. CRICKET. But darling, you must be careful—When you're expecting—And now open the peephole—look—How do you like it?

MRS. CRICKET. Oh, darling, how tired I am!

MR. CRICKET. Sit down, darling, sit down. My popsy must take great care of herself.

MRS. CRICKET. What a long way—And all the move! Oh, men never know half the trouble moving is.

MR. CRICKET. Oh darling, come, come—Look, darling, look.

MRS. CRICKET. Now don't get cross, you horrid man.

MR. CRICKET. I won't say another word, really I won't. Fancy, Mrs. Cricket won't take care of herself, and in her state too—What do you think of her?

MRS. CRICKET. You naughty man—how can you joke about it?

MR. CRICKET. But darling, I'm so happy. Just fancy, all the little crickets, the noise, the chirping—

[*Imitates the noise and laughs.*

MRS. CRICKET. You—you silly boy—wants to be a great big Daddy, eh?

MR. CRICKET. And don't you want to be a Mummy too?—my Popsy?

MRS. CRICKET. Yes'm does! Is this our new home?

MR. CRICKET. Our little nest. Commodious little villa residence.

MRS. CRICKET. Will it be dry? Who built it?

MR. CRICKET. Why, goodness me, another Cricket lived here years ago.

MRS. CRICKET. Fancy, and has he moved?

MR. CRICKET. Ha, ha—Yes, he's moved. Don't you know where to? Guess.

MRS. CRICKET. I don't know—What a long time you take saying anything—Do tell me, Cricket, quickly.

MR. CRICKET. Well, yesterday a bird got him—Snap, snip, snap. So we're moving into his house. By jove, what a slice of luck!

MRS. CRICKET. Gobbled him up alive? How horrible!

MR. CRICKET. Eh? A godsend for us. I did laugh. Tralala, &c. We'll put up a plate. [*Puts up plate with 'Mr. Cricket, musician'.*] Where shall we put it? More to the right? Higher?

MRS. CRICKET. And you saw him eaten?

MR. CRICKET. I'm telling you—like that—snap, snip!

MRS. CRICKET. Horrible! Cricket, I have such a queer feeling.

MR. CRICKET. Good heavens—Perhaps it's—no, it couldn't be, not yet!

MRS. CRICKET. Oh dear, I'm so frightened.

MR. CRICKET. Nothing to be frightened of, dear—Every lady——

MRS. CRICKET. It's all very well for you to talk—Cricket, will you always love me?

MR. CRICKET. Of course, darling—Dear me, don't cry—come, love.

MRS. CRICKET. Show me how he swallowed him—Snip, snap.

MR. CRICKET. Snip, snap.

MRS. CRICKET. Oh, how funny!   [*Has hysterics.*

MR. CRICKET. Well, well. There's nothing to cry about. [*Sits beside her.*] We'll furnish this place beautifully. And as soon as we can run to it, we'll put up some—

MRS. CRICKET. Curtains?

MR. CRICKET. Curtains, of course! How clever of you to think of it. Give me a kiss.

MRS. CRICKET. Never mind that now—Don't be silly.

MR. CRICKET. Of course I'm silly. Guess what I've brought?

MRS. CRICKET. Curtains!

MR. CRICKET. No, something smaller—Where did I—

MRS. CRICKET. Quick, quick, let me see. [MR. CRICKET *takes out a rattle*.] Oh, how sweet, Cricket! Give it to me.

MR. CRICKET [*sings*].

> When Dr. Stork had brought their child,
>   Their teeny-weeny laddy,
> All day about the cradle smiled
>   His mumsy and his daddy:
> And 'Cricket, cricket, cricket,
>   You pretty little thing'—
> Is now the song that all day long
>   They sing, sing, sing.

MRS. CRICKET. Lend it me, darling—Oh, daddy—I'm so pleased. Rattle it.

MR.CRICKET. Darling.

MRS. CRICKET [*singing*]

> Cricket, Cricket, Cricket!

MR. CRICKET. Now I must run round a little—let people know I am here.

MRS. CRICKET [*singing*].

> And 'Cricket, cricket, cricket,
>   You pretty little thing. . . .'

MR. CRICKET. I must get some introductions, fix up orders, have a look round. Give me the rattle, I'll use it on my way.

MRS. CRICKET. And what about me? I want it.

MR. CRICKET. Very well, darling.

MRS. CRICKET. You won't leave me long——

MR. CRICKET. Rattle for me if you want me. And I expect a neighbour will be coming along. Have a chat with him, about the children, and all that, you know.

MRS. CRICKET. You bad boy.

MR. CRICKET. Now darling, be careful. Won't be long, my pet.
[*Runs off.*]

MRS. CRICKET [*rattles*]. Hush-a-bye—cricket—on the tree top!
Cricket! I feel frightened.

TRAMP. Don't be frightened, mum. You'll 'ave an easier time
than most ladies, by the look of yer.

MRS. CRICKET. Who's there, a beetle?—You don't bite?

TRAMP. No.

MRS. CRICKET. And how are the children?

TRAMP. Ah,—now you're askin'! Rum, 'ow
        Yer question 'urts me, some'ow;
        For, beg your pardon, Madam—
        Fact is, I've never 'ad 'em.

MRS. CRICKET. Oh, dear, haven't you any children? That's a
pity. [*Shakes rattle.*] Cricket! Cricket! And why did you
never marry, beetle?

TRAMP. Well, some 's too selfish, maybe,
        To want a wife and baby . . .
        Oh, 'strewth, what do I care now?—
        She wouldn't 'ave me! There now.

MRS. CRICKET. Yes! Yes! You men *are* troublesome. [*Rattles.*]
Cricket! Cricket! Cricket!

CHRYSALIS. In me, in me, in me,
        The future strives to be!

TRAMP. Oh, buck up!

CHRYSALIS. I will accomplish such deeds.

Enter MRS. BEETLE

MRS. BEETLE. Isn't my husband here? Oh, the stupid man.
Where is our pile?

MRS. CRICKET. Your pile? Can we play with it? Do let me see it.

MRS. BEETLE. It's nothing to play with; it's our future, our nest-
egg, our capital. My husband, the clumsy creature, has gone
off with it.

MRS. CRICKET. Oh dear, I hope he hasn't run away from *you*.

THE INSECT PLAY

Produced by The People's National Theatre. Hon. Director: Nancy Price

(Symbolism in Costume)

MRS. BEETLE. And where is yours?

MRS. CRICKET. He's away on business. Cricket! Cricket!

MRS. BEETLE. Fancy him leaving you all alone like that, poor thing, and you—[*Whispers*]—aren't you?

MRS. CRICKET. Oh dear!

MRS. BEETLE. So young, too. And aren't you making a pile?

MRS. CRICKET. What for?

MRS. BEETLE. A pile—for you and him and your family. That's for your future—for your whole life.

MRS. CRICKET. Oh no, all I want is to have my own little home, my nest, a little house of my very own. And curtains, and children, and my Cricket. That's all.

MRS. BEETLE. How can you live without a pile?

MRS. CRICKET. What should I do with it?

MRS. BEETLE. Roll it about with you everywhere. There's nothing like a pile for holding a man.

MRS. CRICKET. Oh, no, a little house.

MRS. BEETLE. A pile, I tell you.

MRS. CRICKET. A little house.

MRS. BEETLE. Pretty little innocence! I'd like to stay with you, but I must be going.

MRS. CRICKET. And I wanted to hear all about your children.

MRS. BEETLE. I don't want to bother over no children. My pile, that's all I want, my pile! [*Exit.*

MRS. CRICKET. Oh, what an old frump! I don't wonder her husband's run away from her. [*Sings a snatch of the song.*] I've such a queer feeling. Snip! Snap! That's what he did to him —Snip!

ICHNEUMON FLY enters

ICHNEUMON FLY. Ha, ha!

[*He murders* MRS. CRICKET *and drags her to his lair.*

TRAMP. Oh, murder!

ICHNEUMON FLY. Daughter, daughter! Chicken! [*Singing.*] 'Open your mouth and shut your eyes and see what some one'll send you.'

TRAMP. 'E's killed 'er, and I stood like a bloomin' log! Didn't utter a sound she didn't, and nobody ran to 'elp her!

Enter PARASITE

PARASITE. Bravo! Comrade, just what I was thinking.

TRAMP. To die—like that—so young, so 'elpless.

PARASITE. Just what I was thinking. I was looking on all the time. I wouldn't do a thing like that, you know. I wouldn't really. Every one wants to live, don't they?

TRAMP. Who are you?

PARASITE. I, oh nothing much, I'm a poor man, an orphan. They call me a parasite.

TRAMP. How can any one dare to kill like that!

PARASITE. That's just what I say. Do you think he needs it? Do you think he's hungry like me? Not a bit of it. He kills to add to his larder, what's three-quarters full already. He collects things he does, hangs 'em up to dry, smokes 'em, pickles 'em. It's a scandal, that's what it is, a scandal. One's got a store while another's starving. Why should he have a dagger, and me only bare fists to fight with, and all over chilblains too—aren't I right?

TRAMP. I should say so.

PARASITE. There's no equality, that's what I say. One law for the rich—another for the poor! And if I was to kill anything, I couldn't eat it—not satisfactorily, I can't chew properly, my jaw's too weak. Is that right?

TRAMP. I don't 'old with killin', no'ow.

PARASITE. My very words, Comrade, or at least, hoarding shouldn't be allowed. Eat your fill and 'ave done with it. Down with larders! Storing things is robbin' those who haven't nowhere to store. Eat your fill and have done with it and then there'd be enough for all, wouldn't there?

TRAMP. I dunno—

PARASITE. Well, I'm tellin' yer, aren't I? Down with——

ICHNEUMON FLY [*re-entering*]. Eat it up, baby, eat it up. Choose what you like. Have you got a nice daddy? Eh?

PARASITE. Good afternoon, my lord.

ICHNEUMON FLY. How d'ye do? Edible?   [*Sniffing.*

PARASITE. Oh no, you're joking, guv'nor; why me?

ICHNEUMON FLY. Get out, you filthy creature. What d'ye want here? Clear off!

PARASITE. I'm movin', your worship; no offence, captain. [*Cowers.*

ICHNEUMON FLY [*to* TRAMP]. Well, did you see that neat piece of work, eh? It's not every one who could do that. Ah, my boy, that's what you want—brains, expert knowledge, enterprise, imagination, initiative—and love of work, let me tell you.

PARASITE. That's what I say.

ICHNEUMON FLY. My good man, if you want to keep alive, you've got to fight your way. There's your future, there's your family. And then you know there must be a certain amount of ambition. A strong personality is bound to assert itself.

PARASITE. That's what I say, sir.

ICHNEUMON FLY. Of course, of course. Make your way in the world. Use the talent that's in you, that's what I call a useful life.

PARASITE. Absolutely, your grace 'its it every time.

ICHNEUMON FLY. Hold your tongue, you filthy creature. I'm not talking to you.

PARASITE. No, of course you weren't, my lord; beg your pardon, I'm sure.

ICHNEUMON FLY. And how it cheers you up when you do your duty like that. 'Do the job that's nearest, though it's dull at whiles.' When you feel that, you feel that you are not living in vain. 'Life is *real*, life is earnest, life is not an empty dream.' Well, good afternoon, sir, I must be off again! 'The daily round, the common task!' So long!   [*Exit.*

PARASITE. The old murderer. Believe me, it was all I could do not to fly at his throat! Yes, sir, I'll work too if need be, but why should I work when somebody else has more than he can consume? I've got initiative—but I keep it here. [*Pats stomach.*] I'm 'ungry, that's what I am, 'ungry, that's a pretty stage of things, isn't it?

TRAMP. Anything for a piece of meat.

PARASITE. That's what I say. Anything for a piece of meat, and the poor man's got nothing. It's against nature. Every one should have enough to eat, eh? Down with work!

TRAMP [*shaking rattle*]. Poor creature, poor creature!

PARASITE. That's it. Every one's got a right to live.

> [*Rattle and chirping in reply.*

MR. CRICKET [*enters, rattling*]. Here I am, my pet, here I am, my darling. Where are you, my precious? Guess what hubby's brought you.

ICHNEUMON FLY [*behind him*]. Aha!

TRAMP. Look out—look out!

PARASITE. Don't interfere, mate—don't get mixed up in it. What must be, must be.

MR. CRICKET. Mummy!

ICHNEUMON FLY [*kills him*]. Larva, look what your kind daddy's bringing you now.

TRAMP. Oh, Gawd in Heaven—'ow can you stand by and see it?

PARASITE. Just what I say. That's the third cricket he's had already, and me nothing. And that's what we poor working men are asked to put up with.

ICHNEUMON FLY [*re-entering*]. No, no, kiddy, I've no time. Daddy must go back to work. Eat, eat, eat. Quiet now, I'll be back in an hour.   [*Exit.*

PARASITE. It's more than I can stand—dirty old profiteer! What injustice! I'll show 'im, that I will. Just you wait! [*Trembling.*] 'E's not coming back, is 'e? Keep cave! I must just 'ave a look.

TRAMP. Thank 'eaven! These 'eathen insec's may be vile,
> But man—man's diff'rent. Folks like me an' you
> Work 'ard, real 'ard, and makes our little pile. . . .
> Blast! I'm all mixed. *That's* what them beetles do.

> It's what I say—*man* 'as ideals and dreams
> And fam'ly love. 'Is purpose—put it plain—
> Is keepin' up the race. . . . 'Ullo, though,—seems
> I've got them crickets fairly on the brain.

> Bold—that's what man is: resolute, yer might s'y.
> If 'e wants more, 'e does 'is neighbour in. . . .
> O 'Ell! That makes 'im like this murd'rous fly. . . .
> But, there you are, 'oo can think straight on gin?

CHRYSALIS. I feel something great—something great.

TRAMP. What jer call great?

CHRYSALIS. To be born, to live!

TRAMP. All right, little chrysalis—I won't desert yer.

PARASITE [*rolling out of the* FLY'S *lair, and hiccoughing*]. Ha, ha, ha! Hup—that—ha, ha, hup—the old miser—hup—kept a larder—hup—for that white-faced daughter of his. Hup—ha, ha. I feel quite—hup—I think I'm going to bust—damn the hiccoughs! It's not every one who'd eat as much as that—hup. I'm not a common man, eh, mate?

TRAMP. And 'ow about the Larva?

PARASITE. Oh, I've gobbled her up too, hup. For what we 'ave received may the—hup.

TRAMP. Gah! Bleedin' Bolshie!

POINTS FOR DISCUSSION

1. What is the aim of the writers of the play in presenting men and women as insects?

2. In what ways are the creatures insects, and in what ways are they men and women?

3. How is the utter futility of lives like those of Mr. and Mrs. Beetle emphasized (*a*) in action; (*b*) in the dialogue?

4. Each of the insects represents one type of person or another. Which of their speeches most clearly characterize (*a*) the Ichneumon Fly; (*b*) the Parasite?

5. What makes the sentimentality of Mr. Cricket seem particularly artificial?

6. What purpose is served by the comments of the Tramp? Whom is he expressing?

7. Who is the idealist in the play? What makes it possible for him to be an idealist? Which passage most emphasizes the futility of his idealism?

8. Which speech in the play makes it quite clear to the audience that in the behaviour of the insects is mirrored their own?

9. This play resembles Greek drama in its concern, not with what happens but with the . . . of what happens. Supply the word which has been omitted from this sentence.

10. The official title of the play is 'And so *ad infinitum*'. What does this phrase mean? How is it illustrated in the play?

11. Compare the moral purpose of this play with that of 'Everyman'. What is the basic difference between them?

12. If you were producing this play with a company new to expressionist drama, what advice would you give to the cast as a whole about their method of acting?

THE PLAYS OF GEORGE BERNARD SHAW

Among the giants of modern drama (and there are several) Bernard Shaw stands alone. He has achieved fame, not only as a dramatist, but as a personality; as some one with whom people may not agree, but whom they will find too stimulating to ignore.

His plays do not fit easily into any of the 'types' into which modern drama is often divided, because they cannot be expressed in terms other than themselves, and some people have coined the adjective 'Shavian' to describe the qualities which seem peculiar to Shaw's work. The coinage is interesting, but it is unfortunate that the word has often been used as the expression of a false attitude towards the writings which it is supposed to describe. When people go to the theatre, the majority of them expect primarily to be entertained; and when Shaw invites them to the theatre, he expects them primarily to think. Expressionist plays encourage people to think by giving them an entirely new point of view, one which is essentially unnatural. Shaw refuses to do this. He has neither the patience of Ibsen, who allowed the facts to speak for themselves, nor the aloofness of the expressionists, who removed themselves to a great distance from the facts. His method is to strip from the facts everything which hides them from the intensity of his intellectual scrutiny, until they stand out in a form quite different from that which has made them familiar. People assume that democracy means 'government of the people, by the people, for the people'. In the speech of Boanerges in *The Apple Cart*, Shaw gives them another viewpoint:

'I talk democracy to these men and women. I tell them that they have the vote, and that theirs is the kingdom and the power and the glory. I say to them, "You are supreme: exercise your power." They say, "That's right: tell us what to do"; and I tell them. I say, "Exercise your vote intelligently by voting for me." And they do. That's democracy; and a splendid thing it is too for putting the right men in the right place.'

If what Boanerges says has any relation to the truth, the belief that parliamentary government is necessarily democratic needs considerable revision; and people are most unwilling to revise their beliefs. It is an uncomfortable process. They attempt to dismiss the revelation of a new point of view as a joke, especially if they can find an excuse in the wit of the dialogue through which the view has been expressed. The adjective 'Shavian' has come to be used by people who regard Shaw's plays as collections of witticisms, instead of what they are: ideas expressed in drama by means of the finest prose dialogue which has been written since Shakespeare.

Saint Joan is a play which stands apart from these misunderstandings, because the problems with which it deals are old problems which have become familiar, and which people are prepared to consider. The story of Joan of Arc is too well known to need recapitulation. The extract is chosen from Scene VI of the play, which presents the trial of Joan at the Bishop's court at Rouen.

SAINT JOAN

By GEORGE BERNARD SHAW

Rouen, 30th May 1431. A great stone hall in the castle, arranged for a trial-at-law, but not a trial-by-jury, the court being the Bishop's court with the Inquisition participating:

hence there are two raised chairs side by side for the Bishop and the Inquisitor as judges. Rows of chairs radiating from them at an obtuse angle are for the canons, the doctors of law and theology, and the Dominican monks, who act as assessors. In the angle is a table for the scribes, with stools. There is also a heavy rough wooden stool for the prisoner. All these are at the inner end of the hall. The further end is open to the courtyard through a row of arches. The court is shielded from the weather by screens and curtains.

Looking down the great hall from the middle of the inner end, the judicial chairs and scribes' table are to the right. The prisoner's stool is to the left. There are arched doors right and left. It is a fine sunshiny May morning.

CAUCHON, *the Bishop, is head of the court, though he allows the* INQUISITOR *to direct its proceedings.* CANON DE COURCELLES *is 'a young priest of thirty', and* DE STOGUMBER *is the English Chaplain.* D'ESTIVET *is the Prosecutor or Promoter.*

LADVENU [*a young but ascetically fine-drawn Dominican who is sitting next* COURCELLES, *on his right*]. But is there any great harm in the girl's heresy? Is it not merely her simplicity? Many saints have said as much as Joan.

THE INQUISITOR [*dropping his blandness and speaking very gravely*]. Brother Martin: if you had seen what I have seen of heresy, you would not think it a light thing even in its most apparently harmless and even lovable and pious origins. Heresy begins with people who are to all appearance better than their neighbours. A gentle and pious girl, or a young man who has obeyed the command of our Lord by giving all his riches to the poor, and putting on the garb of poverty, the life of austerity, and the rule of humility and charity, may be the founder of a heresy that will wreck both Church and Empire if not ruthlessly stamped out in time. The records of the holy Inquisition are full of histories we dare not give to the world, because they are beyond the belief of honest men and innocent women; yet they all began with saintly simpletons. I have seen this again and again. Mark what I say: the woman who

SAINT JOAN
Produced by Mary Moore *and* Sybil Thorndike
(Stage grouping on different levels)

quarrels with her clothes, and puts on the dress of a man, is like the man who throws off his fur gown and dresses like John the Baptist: they are followed, as surely as the night follows the day, by bands of wild women and men who refuse to wear any clothes at all. When maids will neither marry nor take regular vows, and men reject marriage and exalt their lusts into divine inspirations, then, as surely as the summer follows the spring, they begin with polygamy, and end by incest. Heresy at first seems innocent and even laudable; but it ends in such a monstrous horror of unnatural wickedness that the most tender-hearted among you, if you saw it at work as I have seen it, would clamor against the mercy of the Church in dealing with it. For two hundred years the Holy Office has striven with these diabolical madnesses; and it knows that they begin always by vain and ignorant persons setting up their own judgment against the Church, and taking it upon themselves to be the interpreters of God's will. You must not fall into the common error of mistaking these simpletons for liars and hypocrites. They believe honestly and sincerely that their diabolical inspiration is divine. Therefore you must be on your guard against your natural compassion. You are all, I hope, merciful men: how else could you have devoted your lives to the service of our gentle Savior? You are going to see before you a young girl, pious and chaste; for I must tell you, gentlemen, that the things said of her by our English friends are supported by no evidence, whilst there is abundant testimony that her excesses have been excesses of religion and charity and not of worldliness and wantonness. This girl is not one of those whose hard features are the sign of hard hearts, and whose brazen looks and lewd demeanor condemn them before they are accused. The devilish pride that has led her into her present peril has left no mark on her countenance. Strange as it may seem to you, it has even left no mark on her character outside those special matters in which she is proud; so that you will see a diabolical pride and a natural humility seated side by side in the selfsame soul. Therefore be on your guard. God forbid that I should tell you to harden your hearts; for her punishment if we condemn her will be so cruel that we should forfeit our own hope of divine mercy were there one grain of malice against her in our hearts. But if you hate cruelty—and if any man here does not hate it I command him on his soul's salvation to quit this holy court—I say, if you hate cruelty, remember that nothing is so cruel in its consequences as the toleration of heresy. Remember also that no court of law can be so cruel as the common people are to those whom they suspect of heresy. The heretic in the hands of the Holy Office is safe from violence, is assured of a fair trial, and cannot suffer death, even when guilty, if repentance follows sin. Innumerable lives of heretics have been saved because the Holy Office has taken them out of the hands of the people, and because the people have yielded them up, knowing that the Holy Office would deal with them. Before the Holy Inquisition existed, and even now when its officers are not within reach, the unfortunate wretch suspected of heresy, perhaps quite ignorantly and unjustly, is stoned, torn in pieces, drowned, burned in his house with all his innocent children, without a trial, unshriven, unburied save as a dog is buried: all of them deeds hateful to God and most cruel to man. Gentlemen: I am compassionate by nature as well as by my profession; and though the work I have to do may seem cruel to those who do not know how much more cruel it would be to leave it undone, I would go to the stake myself sooner than do it if I did not know its righteousness, its necessity, its essential mercy. I ask you to address yourself to this trial in that conviction. Anger is a bad counsellor: cast out anger. Pity is sometimes worse: cast out pity. But do not cast out mercy. Remember only that justice comes first. Have you anything to say, my lord, before we proceed to trial?

CAUCHON. You have spoken for me, and spoken better than I could. I do not see how any sane man could disagree with a word that has fallen from you. But this I will add. The crude heresies of which you have told us are horrible; but their horror is like that of the black death: they rage for a while and then die out, because sound and sensible men will not under any incitement be reconciled to nakedness and incest and polygamy and the like. But we are confronted today throughout Europe with a heresy that is spreading among men not weak in mind nor diseased in brain: nay, the stronger the mind, the more obstinate the heretic. It is neither discredited by fantastic extremes nor corrupted by the common lusts of the flesh; but it, too, sets up the private judgment of the single erring mortal against the considered wisdom and experience of the Church. The mighty structure of Catholic Christendom will never be shaken by naked madmen or by the sins of Moab and Ammon. But it may be betrayed from within, and brought to barbarous ruin and desolation, by this arch heresy which the English Commander calls Protestantism.

THE ASSESSORS [*whispering*]. Protestantism! What was that! What does the Bishop mean? Is it a new heresy? The English Commander, he said. Did you ever hear of Protestantism? etc., etc.

CAUCHON [*continuing*]. And that reminds me. What provision has the Earl of Warwick made for the defence of the secular arm should The Maid prove obdurate, and the people be moved to pity her?

THE CHAPLAIN. Have no fear on that score, my lord. The noble earl has eight hundred men-at-arms at the gates. She will not slip through our English fingers even if the whole city be on her side.

CAUCHON [*revolted*]. Will you not add, God grant that she repent and purge her sin?

THE CHAPLAIN. That does not seem to me to be consistent; but of course I agree with your lordship.

CAUCHON [*giving him up with a shrug of contempt*]. The court sits.

THE INQUISITOR. Let the accused be brought in.

LADVENU [*calling*]. The accused. Let her be brought in.

    [JOAN, *chained by the ankles, is brought in through the arched door behind the prisoner's stool by a guard of English soldiers.*

With them is THE EXECUTIONER *and his assistants. They lead her to the prisoner's stool, and place themselves behind it after taking off her chain. She wears a page's black suit. Her long imprisonment and the strain of the examinations which have preceded the trial have left their mark on her; but her vitality still holds: she confronts the court unabashed, without a trace of the awe which their formal solemnity seems to require for the complete success of its impressiveness.*

THE INQUISITOR [*kindly*]. Sit down, Joan. [*She sits on the prisoner's stool.*] You look very pale today. Are you not well?

JOAN. Thank you kindly: I am well enough. But the Bishop sent me some carp; and it made me ill.

CAUCHON. I am sorry. I told them to see that it was fresh.

JOAN. You meant to be good to me, I know; but it is a fish that does not agree with me. The English thought you were trying to poison me——

CAUCHON   } [*together*] { What!
THE CHAPLAIN }   { No, my lord.

JOAN [*continuing*]. They are determined that I shall be burnt as a witch; and they sent their doctor to cure me; but he was forbidden to bleed me because the silly people believe that a witch's witchery leaves her if she is bled: so he only called me filthy names. Why do you leave me in the hands of the English? I should be in the hands of the Church. And why must I be chained by the feet to a log of wood? Are you afraid I will fly away?

D'ESTIVET [*harshly*]. Woman: it is not for you to question the court: it is for us to question you.

COURCELLES. When you were left unchained, did you not try to escape by jumping from a tower sixty feet high? If you cannot fly like a witch, how is it that you are still alive?

JOAN. I suppose because the tower was not so high then. It has grown higher every day since you began asking me questions about it.

D'ESTIVET. Why did you jump from the tower?

JOAN. How do you know that I jumped?

D'ESTIVET. You were found lying in the moat. Why did you leave the tower?

JOAN. Why would anybody leave a prison if they could get out?

D'ESTIVET. You tried to escape?

JOAN. Of course I did; and not for the first time either. If you leave the door of the cage open the bird will fly out.

D'ESTIVET [*rising*]. That is a confession of heresy. I call the attention of the court to it.

JOAN. Heresy, he calls it! Am I a heretic because I try to escape from prison?

D'ESTIVET. Assuredly, if you are in the hands of the Church, and you wilfully take yourself out of its hands, you are deserting the Church; and that is heresy.

JOAN. It is great nonsense. Nobody could be such a fool as to think that.

D'ESTIVET. You hear, my lord, how I am reviled in the execution of my duty by this woman.   [*He sits down indignantly.*

CAUCHON. I have warned you before, Joan, that you are doing yourself no good by these pert answers.

JOAN. But you will not talk sense to me. I am reasonable if you will be reasonable.

THE INQUISITOR [*interposing*]. This is not yet in order. You forget, Master Promoter, that the proceedings have not been formally opened. The time for questions is after she has sworn on the Gospels to tell us the whole truth.

JOAN. You say this to me every time. I have said again and again that I will tell you all that concerns this trial. But I cannot tell you the whole truth: God does not allow the whole truth to be told. You do not understand it when I tell it. It is an old saying that he who tells too much truth is sure to be hanged. I am weary of this argument: we have been over it nine times already. I have sworn as much as I will swear; and I will swear no more.

COURCELLES. My lord: she should be put to the torture.

THE INQUISITOR. You hear, Joan? That is what happens to the obdurate. Think before you answer. Has she been shewn the instruments?

THE EXECUTIONER. They are ready, my lord. She has seen them.

JOAN. If you tear me limb from limb until you separate my soul from my body you will get nothing out of me beyond what I have told you. What more is there to tell that you could understand? Besides, I cannot bear to be hurt; and if you hurt me I will say anything you like to stop the pain. But I will take it all back afterwards; so what is the use of it?

LADVENU. There is much in that. We should proceed mercifully.

COURCELLES. But the torture is customary.

THE INQUISITOR. It must not be applied wantonly. If the accused will confess voluntarily, then its use cannot be justified.

COURCELLES. But this is unusual and irregular. She refuses to take the oath.

LADVENU [*disgusted*]. Do you want to torture the girl for the mere pleasure of it?

COURCELLES [*bewildered*]. But it is not a pleasure. It is the law. It is customary. It is always done.

THE INQUISITOR. That is not so, Master, except when the inquiries are carried on by people who do not know their legal business.

COURCELLES. But the woman is a heretic. I assure you it is always done.

CAUCHON [*decisively*]. It will not be done today if it is not necessary. Let there be an end of this. I will not have it said that we proceeded on forced confessions. We have sent our best preachers and doctors to this woman to exhort and implore her to save her soul and body from the fire: we shall not now send the executioner to thrust her into it.

COURCELLES. Your lordship is merciful, of course. But it is a great responsibility to depart from the usual practice.

JOAN. Thou art a rare noodle, Master. Do what was done last time is thy rule, eh?

COURCELLES [*rising*]. Thou wanton: dost thou dare call me noodle?

THE INQUISITOR. Patience, Master, patience: I fear you will soon be only too terribly avenged.

COURCELLES [*mutters*]. Noodle indeed!

[*He sits down, much discontented.*

THE INQUISITOR. Meanwhile, let us not be moved by the rough side of a shepherd lass's tongue.

JOAN. Nay: I am no shepherd lass, though I have helped with the sheep like anyone else. I will do a lady's work in the house—spin or weave—against any woman in Rouen.

THE INQUISITOR. This is not a time for vanity, Joan. You stand in great peril.

JOAN. I know it: have I not been punished for my vanity? If I had not worn my cloth of gold surcoat in battle like a fool, that Burgundian soldier would never have pulled me backwards off my horse; and I should not have been here.

THE CHAPLAIN. If you are so clever at woman's work why do you not stay at home and do it?

JOAN. There are plenty of other women to do it; but there is nobody to do my work.

CAUCHON. Come! we are wasting time on trifles. Joan: I am going to put a most solemn question to you. Take care how you answer; for your life and salvation are at stake on it. Will you for all you have said and done, be it good or bad, accept the judgment of God's Church on earth? More especially as to the acts and words that are imputed to you in this trial by the Promoter here, will you submit your case to the inspired interpretation of the Church Militant?

JOAN. I am a faithful child of the Church. I will obey the Church—

CAUCHON [*hopefully leaning forward*]. You will?

JOAN. —provided it does not command anything impossible.

[CAUCHON *sinks back in his chair with a heavy sigh. The* INQUISITOR *purses his lips and frowns.* LADVENU *shakes his head pitifully.*

D'ESTIVET. She imputes to the Church the error and folly of commanding the impossible.

JOAN. If you command me to declare that all that I have done and said, and all the visions and revelations I have had, were not from God, then that is impossible: I will not declare it for anything in the world. What God made me do I will never go back on; and what He has commanded or shall command I will not fail to do in spite of any man alive. That is what I mean by impossible. And in case the Church should bid me do anything contrary to the command I have from God, I will not consent to it, no matter what it may be.

THE ASSESSORS [*shocked and indignant*]. Oh! The Church contrary to God! What do you say now? Flat heresy. This is beyond everything, etc., etc.

D'ESTIVET [*throwing down his brief*]. My lord: do you need anything more than this?

CAUCHON. Woman: you have said enough to burn ten heretics. Will you not be warned? Will you not understand?

THE INQUISITOR. If the Church Militant tells you that your revelations and visions are sent by the devil to tempt you to your damnation, will you not believe that the Church is wiser than you?

JOAN. I believe that God is wiser than I; and it is His commands that I will do. All the things that you call my crimes have come to me by the command of God. I say that I have done them by the order of God: it is impossible for me to say anything else. If any Churchman says the contrary I shall not mind him: I shall mind God alone, whose command I always follow.

LADVENU [*pleading with her urgently*]. You do not know what you are saying, child. Do you want to kill yourself? Listen. Do you not believe that you are subject to the Church of God on earth?

JOAN. Yes. When have I ever denied it?

LADVENU. Good. That means, does it not, that you are subject to our Lord the Pope, to the cardinals, the archbishops, and the bishops for whom his lordship stands here today?

JOAN. God must be served first.

D'ESTIVET. Then your voices command you not to submit yourself to the Church Militant?

JOAN. My voices do not tell me to disobey the Church; but God must be served first.

CAUCHON. And you, and not the Church, are to be the judge?

JOAN. What other judgment can I judge by but my own?

THE ASSESSORS [*scandalized*]. Oh! [*They cannot find words.*

CAUCHON. Out of your own mouth you have condemned yourself. We have striven for your salvation to the verge of sinning ourselves: we have opened the door to you again and again; and you have shut it in our faces and in the face of God. Dare you pretend, after what you have said, that you are in a state of grace?

JOAN. If I am not, may God bring me to it: if I am, may God keep me in it!

LADVENU. That is a very good reply, my lord.

COURCELLES. Were you in a state of grace when you stole the Bishop's horse?

CAUCHON [*rising in a fury*]. Oh, devil take the Bishop's horse and you too! We are here to try a case of heresy; and no sooner do we come to the root of the matter than we are thrown back by idiots who understand nothing but horses.

[*Trembling with rage, he forces himself to sit down.*

THE INQUISITOR. Gentlemen, gentlemen: in clinging to these small issues you are The Maid's best advocates. I am not surprised that his lordship has lost patience with you. What does the Promoter say? Does he press these trumpery matters?

D'ESTIVET. I am bound by my office to press everything; but when the woman confesses a heresy that must bring upon her the doom of excommunication, of what consequence is it that she has been guilty also of offences which expose her to minor penances? I share the impatience of his lordship as to these minor charges. Only, with great respect, I must emphasize the gravity of two very horrible and blasphemous crimes which she does not deny. First, she has intercourse with evil spirits, and is therefore a sorceress. Second, she wears men's clothes, which is indecent, unnatural, and abominable; and in spite of our most earnest remonstrances and entreaties, she will not change them even to receive the sacrament.

JOAN. Is the blessed St. Catherine an evil spirit? Is St. Margaret? Is Michael the Archangel?

COURCELLES. How do you know that the spirit which appears to you is an archangel? Does he not appear to you as a naked man?

JOAN. Do you think God cannot afford clothes for him?

> [*The assessors cannot help smiling, especially as the joke is against* COURCELLES.

LADVENU. Well answered, Joan.

THE INQUISITOR. It is, in effect, well answered. But no evil spirit would be so simple as to appear to a young girl in a guise that would scandalize her when he meant her to take him for a messenger from the Most High. Joan: the Church instructs you that these apparitions are demons seeking your soul's perdition. Do you accept the instruction of the Church?

JOAN. I accept the messenger of God. How could any faithful believer in the Church refuse him?

CAUCHON. Wretched woman: again, I ask you, do you know what you are saying?

THE INQUISITOR. You wrestle in vain with the devil for her soul, my lord: she will not be saved.

POINTS FOR DISCUSSION

1. Which speech expresses the attitude of the audience towards Joan's eccentricities?

2. It is a commonplace to say that long speeches in plays are 'undramatic'. What is meant by this statement?

3. The Inquisitor's speech at the beginning of the extract is one of the longest in modern drama, and yet it is intensely interesting, on the stage, as well as in the study. Why is this?

4. Imagine that you are producing *Saint Joan*, and complete the following statement, addressed to the actors. 'No matter how well the Inquisitor's speech is delivered, it will lose the greater part of its effect if. . . .'

5. How is the scrupulous fairness of the Inquisitor and Cauchon towards Joan emphasized, apart from what they say in their speeches?

6. What is the dramatic purpose of the talk about the carp when Joan enters, and of her display of vanity when the Inquisitor calls her a shepherd lass?

7. To what class of person does Courcelles belong?

8. Which character is it whose presence on the stage shows the fundamental difference between the outlook of the Inquisitor and that of the modern church? What is the difference?

9. What was Joan's heresy? Which speech in the play puts it most clearly?

10. What are the arguments for and against the suggestion that, in this scene, *Saint Joan* becomes a tragedy?

CHAPTER VII

THE MODERN STAGE II

THE RETURN OF VERSE DRAMA

ONE of the characteristics of the modern stage has been the willingness of audiences to enjoy the unfamiliar and the un-expected. The majority of plays with a successful run have continued to be written within the convention of naturalism, yet some of the most strikingly successful have created their own conventions without in any way pretending to mirror the life of everyday experience. In the early nineteen thirties it would have seemed difficult to devise a surer recipe for theatrical failure than a play written in verse on a religious theme making use of conventions from classical drama. It is hardly likely that such a play would ever have been written but for the Canterbury Festival of 1935, at which Martin Browne produced *Murder in the Cathedral*, a play by T. S. Eliot taking for its theme the martyrdom of Archbishop Thomas Becket. Even after its success at the Festival and with some alterations to make it more suitable for the stage the play seemed to be a commercial risk and was produced at the Mercury, one of the small 'intimate' London theatres. Its success there led to productions on a much bigger scale.

Part of the success of *Murder in the Cathedral* was due to the re-discovery of the effectiveness of dramatic conventions that had long been abandoned. The contribution of a Chorus, commenting on and creating the mood of the action, and the cadences of choral verse-speaking came as a revelation of delight to audiences to whom they were unfamiliar. Through-out the play the rhythm of the verse gave a quality to the dialogue that chimed perfectly with its theme and made the sudden descent into prose at the conclusion a most powerful means of bringing home to the audience the contemporary meaning of a play which analyses human motive and examines the significance of action.

None of Eliot's subsequent plays in verse has had quite the success of his first, but his plays, with those of Auden, Isherwood, and Fry have re-established verse drama in the contemporary theatre.

The extract begins after the Four Knights have already appeared once with their murderous intent clearly apparent, and the priests of the Cathedral are attempting to bar the door against their return.

MURDER IN THE CATHEDRAL
By T. S. ELIOT

PRIESTS

Bar the door. Bar the door.
The door is barred.
We are safe. We are safe.
They dare not break in.
They cannot break in. They have not the force.
We are safe. We are safe.

THOMAS

Unbar the doors! throw open the doors!
I will not have the house of prayer, the church of Christ,
The sanctuary, turned into a fortress.
The Church shall protect her own, in her own way, not
As oak and stone; stone and oak decay,
Give no stay, but the Church shall endure.
The church shall be open, even to our enemies. Open the door!

PRIEST

My Lord! these are not men, these come not as men come, but
Like maddened beasts. They come not like men, who

Respect the sanctuary, who kneel to the Body of Christ,
But like beasts. You would bar the door
Against the lion, the leopard, the wolf or the boar,
Why not more
Against beasts with the souls of damned men, against men
Who would damn themselves to beasts. My Lord! My Lord!

THOMAS

You think me reckless, desperate and mad.
You argue by results, as this world does,
To settle if an act be good or bad.
You defer to the fact. For every life and every act
Consequence of good and evil can be shown.
And as in time results of many deeds are blended
So good and evil in the end become confounded.
It is not in time that my death shall be known;
It is out of time that my decision is taken
If you call that decision
To which my whole being gives entire consent.
I give my life
To the Law of God above the Law of Man.
Unbar the door! unbar the door!
We are not here to triumph by fighting, by stratagem, or by resis-
tance.
Not to fight with beasts as men. We have fought the beast
And have conquered. We have only to conquer
Now, by suffering. This is the easier victory.
Now is the triumph of the Cross, now
Open the door! I command it. OPEN THE DOOR!

[The door is opened. The KNIGHTS *enter, slightly tipsy.*

PRIESTS

This way, my Lord! Quick. Up the stair. To the roof.
To the crypt. Quick. Come. Force him.

KNIGHTS

Where is Becket, the traitor to the King?
Where is Becket, the meddling priest?

Come down Daniel to the lions' den,
  Come down Daniel for the mark of the beast.

Are you washed in the blood of the Lamb?
Are you marked with the mark of the beast?
Come down Daniel to the lions' den,
  Come down Daniel and join in the feast.

Where is Becket the Cheapside brat?
  Where is Becket the faithless priest?
Come down Daniel to the lions' den,
Come down Daniel and join in the feast.

THOMAS

It is the just man who
Like a bold lion, should be without fear.
I am here.
No traitor to the King. I am a priest,
A Christian, saved by the blood of Christ,
Ready to suffer with my blood.
This is the sign of the Church always,
The sign of blood. Blood for blood.
His blood given to buy my life,
My blood given to pay for His death,
My death or His death.

FIRST KNIGHT

Absolve all those you have excommunicated.

SECOND KNIGHT

Resign the powers you have arrogated.

THIRD KNIGHT

Restore to the King the money you appropriated.

FIRST KNIGHT

Renew the obedience you have violated.

THOMAS

For my Lord I am now ready to die,
That His Church may have peace and liberty.
Do with me as you will, to your hurt and shame;
But none of my people, in God's name,
Whether layman or clerk, shall you touch.
This I forbid.

KNIGHTS

Traitor! traitor! traitor!

THOMAS

You, Reginald, three times traitor you:
Traitor to me as my temporal vassal,
Traitor to me as your spiritual lord,
Traitor to God in desecrating His Church.

FIRST KNIGHT

No faith do I owe to a renegrade,
And what I owe shall now be paid.

THOMAS

Now to Almighty God, to the Blessed Mary ever Virgin, to the
blessed John the Baptist, the holy apostles Peter and Paul, to the
blessed martyr Denys, and to all the Saints, I commend my cause
and that of the Church.

[*While the* KNIGHTS *kill him, we hear the*
CHORUS OF WOMEN OF CANTERBURY.

Clear the air! clean the sky! wash the wind! take stone from stone
and wash them.
The land is foul, the water is foul, our beasts and ourselves defiled
with blood.
A rain of blood has blinded my eyes. Where is England?
where is Kent? where is Canterbury?
O far far far in the past; and I wander in a land of barren boughs:
if I break them, they bleed; I wander in a land of dry stones: if
I touch them they bleed.

MURDER IN THE CATHEDRAL
Old Vic Production by Robert Helpmann
(Stylized acting)

How how can I ever return, to the soft quiet seasons?

Night stay with us, stop sun, hold season, let the day not come,
let the spring not come.

Can I look again at the day and its common things, and see them
all smeared with blood, through a curtain of falling blood?

We did not wish anything to happen.

We understood the private catastrophe,

The personal loss, the general misery,

Living and partly living;

The terror by night that ends in daily action,

The terror by day that ends in sleep;

But the talk in the market-place, the hand on the broom,

The night-time heaping of the ashes,

The fuel laid on the fire at daybreak,

These acts marked a limit to our suffering.

Every horror had its definition,

Every sorrow had a kind of end:

In life there is not time to grieve long.

But this, this is out of life, this is out of time,

An instant eternity of evil and wrong.

We are soiled by a filth that we cannot clean, united to supernatural
vermin,

It is not we alone, it is not the house, it is not the city that is
defiled,

But the world that is wholly foul.

Clear the air! clean the sky! wash the wind! take the stone from
the stone, take the skin from the arm, take the muscle from the
bone, and wash them. Wash the stone, wash the bone, wash
the brain, wash the soul, wash them wash them!

[*The* KNIGHTS, *having completed the murder, advance to the
front of the stage and address the audience.*

FIRST KNIGHT

We beg you to give us your attention for a few moments. We
know that you may be disposed to judge unfavourably of our action.
You are Englishmen, and therefore you believe in fair play: and

when you see one man being set upon by four, then your sympathies are all with the under dog. I respect such feelings, I share them. Nevertheless, I appeal to your sense of honour. You are Englishmen, and therefore will not judge anybody without hearing both sides of the case. That is in accordance with our long-established principle of Trial by Jury. I am not myself qualified to put our case to you. I am a man of action and not of words. For that reason I shall do no more than introduce the other speakers, who, with their various abilities, and different points of view, will be able to lay before you the merits of this extremely complex problem. I shall call upon our eldest member to speak first, my neighbour in the country: Baron William de Traci.

THIRD KNIGHT

I am afraid I am not anything like such an experienced speaker as my old friend Reginald Fitz Urse would lead you to believe. But there is one thing I should like to say, and I might as well say it at once. It is this: in what we have done, and whatever you may think of it, we have been perfectly disinterested. [*The other* KNIGHTS: 'Hear! hear!'.] *We* are not getting anything out of this. We have much more to lose than to gain. We are four plain Englishmen who put our country first. I dare say that we didn't make a very good impression when we came in just now. The fact is that we knew we had taken on a pretty stiff job; I'll only speak for myself, but I had drunk a good deal—I am not a drinking man ordinarily—to brace myself up for it. When you come to the point, it does go against the grain to kill an Archbishop, especially when you have been brought up in good Church traditions. So if we seemed a bit rowdy, you will understand why it was; and for my part I am awfully sorry about it. We realized that this was our duty, but all the same we had to work ourselves up to it. And, as I said, *we* are not getting a penny out of this. We know perfectly well how things will turn out. King Henry—God bless him— will have to say, for reasons of state, that he never meant this to happen; and there is going to be an awful row; and at the best we shall have to spend the rest of our lives abroad. And even when reasonable people come to see that the Archbishop *had* to be put out of the way—and personally I had a tremendous admiration for him—you must have noticed what a good show he put up at the end—they won't give *us* any glory. No, we have done for ourselves, there's no mistake about that. So, as I said at the beginning, please give us at least the credit for being completely disinterested in this business. I think that is about all I have to say.

FIRST KNIGHT

I think we will all agree that William de Traci has spoken well and has made a very important point. The gist of his argument is this: that we have been completely disinterested. But our act itself needs more justification than that; and you must hear our other speakers. I shall next call upon Hugh de Morville, who has made a special study of statecraft and constitutional law. Sir Hugh de Morville.

SECOND KNIGHT

I should like first to recur to a point that was very well put by our leader, Reginald Fitz Urse: that you are Englishmen, and therefore your sympathies are always with the under dog. It is the English spirit of fair play. Now the worthy Archbishop, whose good qualities I very much admired, has throughout been presented as the under dog. But is this really the case? I am going to appeal not to your emotions but to your reason. You are hard-headed sensible people, as I can see, and not to be taken in by emotional clap-trap. I therefore ask you to consider soberly: what were the Archbishop's aims? and what are King Henry's aims? In the answer to these questions lies the key to the problem.

The King's aim has been perfectly consistent. During the reign of the late Queen Matilda and the irruption of the unhappy usurper Stephen, the kingdom was very much divided. Our King saw that the one thing needful was to restore order: to curb the excessive powers of local government, which were usually exercised for selfish and often for seditious ends, and to reform the legal system. He therefore intended that Becket, who had proved himself an extremely able administrator—no one denies that— should unite the offices of Chancellor and Archbishop. Had Becket concurred with the King's wishes, we should have had an almost ideal State: a union of spiritual and temporal administration, under the central government. I knew Becket well, in various official relations; and I may say that I have never known a man so well qualified for the highest rank of the Civil Service. And what happened? The moment that Becket, at the King's instance, had been made Archbishop, he resigned the office of Chancellor, he became more priestly than the priests, he ostentatiously and offensively adopted an ascetic manner of life, he affirmed immediately that there was a higher order than that which our King, and he as the King's servant, had for so many years striven to establish; and that—God knows why—the two orders were incompatible.

You will agree with me that such interference by an Archbishop offends the instincts of a people like ours. So far, I know that I have your approval: I read it in your faces. It is only with the measures we have had to adopt, in order to set matters to rights, that you take issue. No one regrets the necessity for violence more than we do. Unhappily, there are times when violence is the only way in which social justice can be secured. At another time, you would condemn an Archbishop by vote of Parliament and execute him formally as a traitor, and no one would have to bear the burden of being called murderer. And at a later time still, even such temperate measures as these would become unnecessary. But, if you have now arrived at a just subordination of the pretensions of the Church to the welfare of the State, remember that it is we who took the first step. We have been instrumental in bringing about the state of affairs that you approve. We have served your interests; we merit your applause; and if there is any guilt whatever in the matter, you must share it with us.

FIRST KNIGHT

Morville has given us a great deal to think about. It seems to me that he has said almost the last word, for those who have been able to follow his very subtle reasoning. We have, however, one more speaker, who has I think another point of view to express. If there are any who are still unconvinced, I think that Richard Brito, coming as he does of a family distinguished for its loyalty to the Church, will be able to convince them. Richard Brito.

FOURTH KNIGHT

The speakers who have preceded me, to say nothing of our leader, Reginald Fitz Urse, have all spoken very much to the point. I have nothing to add along their particular lines of argument. What I have to say may be put in the form of a question: *Who killed the Archbishop?* As you have been eye-witnesses of this lamentable scene, you may feel some surprise at my putting it in this way. But consider the course of events. I am obliged, very briefly, to go over the ground traversed by the last speaker. While the late Archbishop was Chancellor, no one, under the King, did more to weld the country together, to give it the unity, the stability, order, tranquillity, and justice that it so badly needed. From the moment he became Archbishop, he completely reversed his policy; he showed himself to be utterly indifferent to the fate of the country, to be, in fact, a monster of egotism. This egotism grew upon him, until it became at last an undoubted mania. I have unimpeachable evidence to the effect that before he left France he clearly prophesied, in the presence of numerous witnesses, that he had not long to live, and that he would be killed in England. He used every means of provocation; from his conduct, step by step, there can be no inference except that he had determined upon a death by martyrdom. Even at the last, he could have given us reason: you have seen how he evaded our questions. And when he had deliberately exasperated us beyond human endurance, he could still have easily escaped; he could have kept himself from us long enough to allow our righteous anger to cool. That was just what he did not wish to happen; he insisted, while we were still inflamed with wrath, that the doors should be opened. Need I say more? I think, with these facts before you, you will unhesitatingly render a verdict of Suicide while of Unsound Mind. It is the only charitable verdict you can give, upon one who was, after all, a great man.

FIRST KNIGHT

Thank you, Brito. I think that there is no more to be said; and
I suggest that you now disperse quietly to your homes. Please be
careful not to loiter in groups at street corners, and do nothing
that might provoke any public outbreak.

[*Exeunt* KNIGHTS.

FIRST PRIEST

O father, father, gone from us, lost to us,
How shall we find you, from what far place
Do you look down on us? You now in Heaven,
Who shall now guide us, protect us, direct us?
After what journey through what further dread
Shall we recover your presence? when inherit
Your strength? The Church lies bereft,
Alone, desecrated, desolated, and the heathen shall build on the
    ruins,
Their world without God. I see it. I see it.

THIRD PRIEST

No. For the Church is stronger for this action,
Triumphant in adversity. It is fortified
By persecution: supreme, so long as men will die for it.
Go, weak sad men, lost erring souls, homeless in earth or heaven.
Go where the sunset reddens the last grey rock
Of Brittany, or the Gates of Hercules.
Go venture shipwreck on the sullen coasts
Where blackamoors make captive Christian men;
Go to the northern seas confined with ice
Where the dead breath makes numb the hand, makes dull the
    brain;
Find the oasis in the desert sun,
Go seek alliance with the heathen Saracen,
To share his filthy rites, and try to snatch
Forgetfulness in his libidinous courts,
Oblivion in the fountain by the date-tree;

Or sit and bite your nails in Aquitaine.
In the small circle of pain within the skull
You still shall tramp and tread one endless round
Of thought, to justify your action to yourselves,
Weaving a fiction which unravels as you weave,
Pacing forever in the hell of make-believe
Which never is belief: this is your fate on earth
And we must think no further of you.

FIRST PRIEST

                              O my lord
The glory of whose new state is hidden from us,
Pray for us of your charity.

SECOND PRIEST

                      Now in the sight of God
Conjoined with all the saints and martyrs gone before you,
Remember us.

THIRD PRIEST

              Let our thanks ascend
To God, who has given us another Saint in Canterbury.

POINTS FOR DISCUSSION

1. What is the function of the priests in this scene?
2. 'You defer to the fact.' What does Thomas mean by this?
3. What contribution is made by the Chorus of the women of Canterbury to the dramatic presentation of the murder of Thomas?
4. Discuss the effectiveness of the apologies made by the Second, Third, and Fourth Knights.
5. Are the arguments of the Knights answered?
6. What do you think is the purpose of the unexpected interruption in the play caused by the apologies?
7. What does the play gain because it is written in verse?
8. Discuss the suggestion that two quite different dramatic conventions are used in this extract. What are they and why are they used?
9. Does the play itself reveal any good that has been achieved by the martyrdom of Thomas?

A DRAMA OF INACTION

The enduring fame of *Hamlet*, one of the greatest plays ever written, is evidence enough that a failure to act can be one form of dramatic action. The plays of Chekhov are largely peopled by characters whose inability to make decisions and act upon them is the theme of the drama. This does not mean that the plays themselves are bereft of action. In *Hamlet* there is murder and suicide, a ghost walks at midnight and there are so many corpses on the stage at the conclusion that a special dramatic device is needed to remove them. In *The Cherry Orchard* Madame Ranevsky may turn away from reality, but reality is still there and the play ends with the sound of the axes in the cherry orchard which her fecklessness has lost for ever.

What distinguishes Beckett's play *Waiting for Godot* from all others is the absence of almost any action of any kind. It leaves the audience exactly where it finds them. Part of its success—and people still wonder how it could possibly have succeeded on the West End stage—was due to the astonishment of the audience that dialogue could continue at all with so little action. The play came to have some of the fascination of a walker on a tight-rope who keeps the audience glued to their seats not by the distance he travels but by the fact that he is there at all. *Waiting for Godot* was able to continue in conditions that would normally cause a play to collapse.

That it did not collapse was due to a number of reasons. The West End production gained much from brilliant acting, but the brilliance of the acting was made possible by the dialogue, which translated the words of Shakespeare into a modern idiom and gave

> to airy nothing
> A local habitation and a name.

Such tricks hath strong imagination
That, if it would be apprehend some joy,
It comprehends some bringer of that joy. . . .

Beckett plays very skilfully on two of the commonest human experiences, uncertainty and expectancy. Uncertainty is a disturbing experience that almost every individual has in his own life, and in the second half of the twentieth century it has become a characteristic of the age. Expectancy, when it is unfulfilled, itself becomes but another form of uncertainty, and it is the transition from one to the other that constitutes what may, for want of a better term, be called the dramatic action of *Waiting for Godot.*

Although in most ways the two plays have little in common, it can be said that *Murder in the Cathedral* appeals to religious certainty and *Waiting for Godot* attracted audiences partly by its religious uncertainty. Although personal faith has declined, people continue to be interested in religion and the Biblical overtones of Beckett's play suggest an area of uncertainty that is widely shared. Godot is not God, but he sounds like God and there are Biblical allusions in the dialogue that give a hazily religious background to the conversation between the two tramps, Estragon and Vladimir, who are on the stage alone for the greater part of the time. During the course of Act I two extraordinary characters appear, Pozzo and Lucky. 'Pozzo drives Lucky by means of a rope passed round his neck, so that Lucky is the first to appear, followed by the rope, which is long enough to allow him to reach the middle of the stage before Pozzo appears. Lucky carries a heavy bag, a folding stool, a picnic basket and a greatcoat. Pozzo a whip.' Pozzo treats Lucky with more contempt and cruelty than an ordinary man would treat an animal. In the second act they reappear, but this time Pozzo is blind, and when he falls down he is unable to get up again.

He is on the ground and has called for help when the extract begins.

WAITING FOR GODOT

By SAMUEL BECKETT

SCENE: *A country road. A tree. Evening.*

VLADIMIR. Let us not waste our time in idle discourse! [*Pause. Vehemently.*] Let us do something, while we have the chance! It is not every day that we are needed. Not indeed that we personally are needed. Others would meet the case equally well, if not better. To all mankind they were addressed, those cries for help still ringing in our ears! But at this place, at this moment of time, all mankind is us, whether we like it or not. Let us make the most of it, before it is too late! Let us represent worthily for once the foul brood to which a cruel fate consigned us! What do you say? [ESTRAGON *says nothing.*] It is true that when with folded arms we weigh the pros and cons we are no less a credit to our species. The tiger bounds to the help of his congeners without the least reflection or else he slinks away into the depths of the thickets. But that is not the question. What are we doing here, *that* is the question. And we are blessed in this, that we happen to know the answer. Yes, in this immense confusion one thing alone is clear. We are waiting for Godot to come——

ESTRAGON. Ah!

POZZO. Help!

VLADIMIR. Or for night to fall. [*Pause.*] We have kept our appointment, and that's an end to that. We are not saints, but we have kept our appointment. How many people can boast as much?

ESTRAGON. Billions.

VLADIMIR. You think so?

ESTRAGON. I don't know.

VLADIMIR. You may be right.

POZZO. Help!

VLADIMIR. What's certain is that the hours are long, under these
  conditions, and constrain us to beguile them with proceedings
  which, how shall I say, which may at first sight seem reasonable
  until they become a habit. You may say it is to prevent our
  reason from foundering. No doubt. But has it not long been
  straying in the night without end of the abyssal depths? That's
  what I sometimes wonder. You follow my reasoning?

ESTRAGON [*aphoristic*]. We all are born mad. Some remain so.

POZZO. Help! I'll pay you!

ESTRAGON. How much?

POZZO. Two shillings!

ESTRAGON. It's not enough.

VLADIMIR. I wouldn't go so far as that.

ESTRAGON. You think it's enough?

VLADIMIR. No, I mean so far as to assert that I was weak in the
  head when I came into the world. But that is not the question.

POZZO. Five shillings!

VLADIMIR. We wait. We are bored. [*He throws up his hand.*] No,
  don't protest, we are bored to death, there's no denying it.
  Good. A diversion comes along and what do we do? We let it
  go to waste. Come, let's get to work! [*He advances towards the
  heap, stops in his stride.*] In an instant all will vanish and we'll
  be alone again, in the midst of nothingness! [*He broods.*]

POZZO. Five shillings!

VLADIMIR. We're coming!

  [*He tries to pull* POZZO *to his feet, fails, tries again, stumbles,
  falls, tries to get up, fails.*

ESTRAGON. What's the matter with you all?

VLADIMIR. Help!

ESTRAGON. I'm going.

VLADIMIR. Don't leave me! They'll kill me!

POZZO. Where am I?

VLADIMIR. Gogo!

POZZO. Help!

VLADIMIR. Help!

ESTRAGON. I'm going.

VLADIMIR. Help me up first. Then we'll go together.

ESTRAGON. You promise?

VLADIMIR. I swear it!

ESTRAGON. And we'll never come back?

VLADIMIR. Never!

ESTRAGON. We'll go to the Pyrenees.

VLADIMIR. Wherever you like.

POZZO. Ten shillings—A pound!

ESTRAGON. I've always wanted to wander in the Pyrenees.

VLADIMIR. You'll wander in them.

ESTRAGON [*recoiling*]. Who belched?

VLADIMIR. Pozzo.

POZZO. Here! Here! Pity!

ESTRAGON. It's revolting!

VLADIMIR. Quick! Give me your hand.

ESTRAGON. I'm going. [*Pause. Louder.*] I'm going.

VLADIMIR. Well, I suppose in the end I'll get up under my own steam. [*He tries, fails.*] In the fullness of time.

ESTRAGON. What's the matter with you?

VLADIMIR. Go to hell.

ESTRAGON. Are you staying there?

VLADIMIR. For the time being.

ESTRAGON. Come on, get up, you'll catch a chill.

VLADIMIR. Don't worry about me.

ESTRAGON. Come on, Didi, don't be pig-headed.

> [*He stretches out his hand which* VLADIMIR *makes haste to seize.*

VLADIMIR. Pull!

> [ESTRAGON *pulls, stumbles, falls. Long silence.*

POZZO. Help!

VLADIMIR. We've arrived.

POZZO. Who are you?

VLADIMIR. We are men.   [*Silence.*

ESTRAGON. Sweet Mother Earth!

VLADIMIR. Can you get up?

ESTRAGON. I don't know.

VLADIMIR. Try.

ESTRAGON. Not now, not now. [*Silence.*

POZZO. What's happened?

VLADIMIR [*violently*]. Will you stop it, you! Pest! He thinks of nothing but himself!

ESTRAGON. What about a little snooze?

VLADIMIR. Did you hear him? He wants to know what happened!

ESTRAGON. Don't mind him. Sleep. [*Silence.*

POZZO. Pity! Pity!

ESTRAGON [*with a start*]. What is it?

VLADIMIR. Were you asleep?

ESTRAGON. I must have been.

VLADIMIR. It's this bastard Pozzo at it again.

ESTRAGON. Tell him to stop it. Kick him in the crotch.

VLADIMIR [*striking Pozzo*]. Will you stop it! Crablouse!

[POZZO *extricates himself with cries of pain and crawls away. Now and then he stops, saws the air blindly, calling for help.* VLADIMIR, *propped on his elbow, observes his retreat.*] He's off! [POZZO *collapses.*] He's down!

ESTRAGON. What do we do now?

VLADIMIR. Perhaps I could crawl to him.

ESTRAGON. Don't leave me!

VLADIMIR. Or I could call to him.

ESTRAGON. Yes, call to him.

VLADIMIR. Pozzo! [*Silence.*] Pozzo! [*Silence.*] No reply.

ESTRAGON. Together.

ESTRAGON.
VLADIMIR. } Pozzo! Pozzo!

VLADIMIR. He moved.

ESTRAGON. Are you sure his name is Pozzo?

VLADIMIR. [*alarmed*]. Mr. Pozzo! Come back! We won't touch you! [*Silence.*

ESTRAGON. We might try him with other names.

VLADIMIR. I'm afraid he's dying.

ESTRAGON. It'd be amusing.

VLADIMIR. What'd be amusing?

ESTRAGON. To try him with other names, one after the other. That'd pass the time. And we'd be bound to hit on the right one sooner or later.

VLADIMIR. I tell you his name is Pozzo.

ESTRAGON. We'll soon see. [*He reflects.*] Abel! Abel!

POZZO. Help!

ESTRAGON. Got it in one!

VLADIMIR. I begin to weary of this motif.

ESTRAGON. Perhaps the other is called Cain. [*He calls.*] Cain! Cain!

POZZO. Help!

ESTRAGON. He's all mankind. [*Silence.*] Look at the little cloud.

VLADIMIR [*raising his eyes*]. Where?

ESTRAGON. There. In the zenith.

VLADIMIR. Well? [*Pause.*] What is there so wonderful about it?
　　　　　　　　　　　　　　　　　　　　　　　　　　[*Silence.*

ESTRAGON. Let's pass on now to something else, do you mind?

VLADIMIR. I was just going to suggest it.

ESTRAGON. But to what?

VLADIMIR. Ah! 　　　　　　　　　　　　　　　　　　[*Silence.*

ESTRAGON. Suppose we got up to begin with.

VLADIMIR. No harm in trying. 　　　　　　　　　　　[*They get up.*

ESTRAGON. Child's play.

VLADIMIR. Simple question of will-power.

ESTRAGON. And now?

POZZO. Help!

ESTRAGON. Let's go.

VLADIMIR. We can't.

ESTRAGON. Why not?

VLADIMIR. We're waiting for Godot.

ESTRAGON. Ah! [*Pause. Despairing.*] What'll we do, what'll we do!

POZZO. Help!

VLADIMIR. What about helping him?

ESTRAGON. What does he want?

VLADIMIR. He wants to get up.

ESTRAGON. Then why doesn't he?

VLADIMIR. He wants us to help him to get up.

ESTRAGON. Then why don't we? What are we waiting for?

> [*They help* POZZO *to his feet, let him go. He falls.*

VLADIMIR. We must hold him. [*They get him up again.* POZZO *sags between them, his arms round their necks.*] He must get used to being erect again. [*To* POZZO.] Feeling better?

POZZO. Who are you?

VLADIMIR. Do you not recognize us?

POZZO. I am blind.   [*Silence.*

ESTRAGON. Perhaps he can see into the future.

VLADIMIR [*to* POZZO]. Since when?

POZZO. I used to have wonderful sight—but are you friends?

ESTRAGON [*laughing noisily*]. He wants to know if we are friends!

VLADIMIR. No, he means friends of his.

ESTRAGON. Well?

VLADIMIR. We've proved we are, by helping him.

ESTRAGON. Exactly. Would we have helped him if we weren't his friends?

VLADIMIR. Possibly.

ESTRAGON. True.

VLADIMIR. Don't let's quibble about that now.

POZZO. You are not highwaymen?

ESTRAGON. Highwaymen! Do we look like highwaymen?

VLADIMIR. Damn it, can't you see the man is blind.

ESTRAGON. Damn it, so he is. [*Pause.*] Or so he says.

POZZO. Don't leave me!

VLADIMIR. No question of it.

ESTRAGON. For the moment.

POZZO. What time is it?

VLADIMIR [*inspecting the sky*]. Seven o'clock—eight o'clock—

ESTRAGON. That depends what time of year it is.

POZZO. Is it evening?

> [*Silence.* VLADIMIR *and* ESTRAGON *scrutinize the sunset.*

ESTRAGON. It looks as if it was rising backwards.

VLADIMIR. Impossible.

ESTRAGON. Perhaps it's the dawn.

VLADIMIR. Don't be a fool. It's the west over there.

ESTRAGON. How do you know?

POZZO [*anguished*]. Is it evening?

VLADIMIR. Anyway, it hasn't moved.

ESTRAGON. I tell you it's rising.

POZZO. Why don't you answer?

ESTRAGON. Give us a chance!

VLADIMIR [*reassuring*]. It's evening, sir, it's evening, night is
  drawing nigh. My friend here would have me doubt it and I must
  confess he shook me for a moment. But it is not for nothing that
  I have lived through this long day and I can assure you it is very
  near the end of its repertory. [*Pause.*] How do you feel now?

ESTRAGON. How much longer must we cart him round? [*They
  half release him, catch him again as he falls.*] We are not carya-
  tides!

VLADIMIR. You were saying that your sight used to be good, if I
  heard you right.

POZZO. Wonderful! Wonderful, wonderful sight!   [*Silence.*

ESTRAGON [*irritably*]. Expand! Expand!

VLADIMIR. Let him alone. Can't you see he's thinking of the
  days when he was happy? [*Pause.*] *Memoria praeteritorum
  bonorum*—that must be unpleasant.

ESTRAGON. We wouldn't know.

VLADIMIR [*to* POZZO]. And it came on you all of a sudden?

POZZO. Quite wonderful?

VLADIMIR. I'm asking you if it came on you all of a sudden.

POZZO. I woke up one fine day as blind as Fortune. [*Pause.*]
  Sometimes I wonder if I'm not still asleep.

VLADIMIR. When was that?

POZZO. I don't know.

VLADIMIR. But no later than yesterday—

POZZO. Don't question me. The blind have no notion of time.
  The things of time are hidden from them too.

VLADIMIR. Well, just fancy that! I could have sworn it was the
  opposite.

ESTRAGON. I'm going.

POZZO. Where are we?

VLADIMIR. I couldn't tell you.

POZZO. It isn't by any chance the place known as the Board?

VLADIMIR. Never heard of it.

POZZO. What is it like?

VLADIMIR [*looking round*]. You couldn't describe it. It's like nothing. There's nothing. There's a tree.

POZZO. Then it's not the Board.

ESTRAGON [*sagging*]. Some diversion!

POZZO. Where is my menial?

VLADIMIR. He's about somewhere.

POZZO. Why doesn't he answer when I call?

VLADIMIR. I don't know. He seems to be sleeping. Perhaps he's dead.

POZZO. What happened exactly?

ESTRAGON. Exactly!

VLADIMIR. The two of you slipped. [*Pause.*] And fell.

POZZO. Go and see is he hurt.

VLADIMIR. But we can't leave you.

POZZO. You needn't both go.

VLADIMIR [*to* ESTRAGON]. You go.

ESTRAGON. After what he did to me? Never!

POZZO. Yes yes, let your friend go, he stinks so. [*Silence*] What is he waiting for?

VLADIMIR. What are you waiting for?

ESTRAGON. I'm waiting for Godot.   [*Silence.*

VLADIMIR. What exactly should he do?

POZZO. Well, to begin with, he should pull on the rope, as hard as he likes so long as he doesn't strangle him. He usually responds to that. If not he should give him a taste of his boot, in the face and the guts as far as possible.

VLADIMIR [*to* ESTRAGON]. You see, you've nothing to be afraid of. It's even an opportunity to revenge yourself.

ESTRAGON. And if he defends himself?

POZZO. No, no, he never defends himself.

VLADIMIR. I'll come flying to the rescue.

ESTRAGON. Don't take your eyes off me.

[*He goes towards* LUCKY.

VLADIMIR. Make sure he's alive before you start. No point in exerting yourself if he's dead.

ESTRAGON [*bending over* LUCKY]. He's breathing.

VLADIMIR. Then let him have it.

[*With sudden fury* ESTRAGON *starts kicking* LUCKY, *hurling abuse at him as he does so. But he hurts his foot and moves away, limping and groaning.* LUCKY *stirs.*

ESTRAGON. Oh, the brute!

[*He sits down on the mound and tries to take off his boots. But he soon desists and disposes himself for sleep, his arms on his knees and his head on his arms.*

POZZO. What's gone wrong now?

VLADIMIR. My friend has hurt himself.

POZZO. And Lucky?

VLADIMIR. So it is he?

POZZO. What?

VLADIMIR. It is Lucky?

POZZO. I don't understand.

VLADIMIR. And you are Pozzo?

POZZO. Certainly I am Pozzo.

VLADIMIR. The same as yesterday?

POZZO. Yesterday?

VLADIMIR. We met yesterday. [*Silence.*] Do you not remember?

POZZO. I don't remember having met anyone yesterday. But tomorrow I won't remember having met anyone today. So don't count on me to enlighten you.

VLADIMIR. But——

POZZO. That's enough. Up, pig!

VLADIMIR. You were bringing him to the fair to sell him. You spoke to us. He danced. He thought. You had your sight.

POZZO. As you please. Let me go. [VLADIMIR *moves aside.*] Up!

[LUCKY *gets up, gathering up his burdens.*

VLADIMIR. Where do you go from here?

POZZO. I don't concern myself with that. On! [LUCKY, *laden*

WAITING FOR GODOT
Arts Theatre Production by Peter Hall

down, takes his place before POZZO.] Whip! [*Lucky puts everything down, looks for the whip, finds it, puts it into* POZZO'S *hand,
takes up everything again.*] Rope!

[LUCKY *puts everything down, puts the end of the rope into*
POZZO'S *hand, takes up everything again.*

VLADIMIR. What is there in the bag?

POZZO. Sand. [*He jerks the rope.*] March!

VLADIMIR. Don't go yet!

POZZO. I'm going.

VLADIMIR. What do you do when you fall far from help?

POZZO. We wait till we can get up. Then we go on. On!

VLADIMIR. Before you go, tell him to sing!

POZZO. Who?

VLADIMIR. Lucky.

POZZO. To sing?

VLADIMIR. Yes. Or to think. Or to recite.

POZZO. But he's dumb.

VLADIMIR. Dumb!

POZZO. Dumb. He can't even groan.

VLADIMIR. Dumb! Since when?

POZZO [*suddenly furious*]. Have you not done tormenting me with
your accursed time? It's abominable. When! When! One
day, is that not enough for you, one day like any other day, one
day he went dumb, one day I went blind, one day we'll go deaf,
one day we were born, one day we'll die, the same day, the same
second, is that not enough for you? [*Calmer.*] They give birth
astride of a grave, the light gleams an instant, then it's night
once more. [*He jerks the rope.*] On!

[*Exeunt* LUCKY *and* POZZO. VLADIMIR *follows them to the
edge of the stage, looks after them. The noise of a fall, re-
inforced by mimic of* VLADIMIR. VLADIMIR *goes towards*
ESTRAGON *who is asleep, announces that they are down again.
Silence. Contemplates him a moment, then shakes him
awake.*

ESTRAGON [*wild gestures, incoherent words. Finally*]. Why will you
never let me sleep?

VLADIMIR. I felt lonely.

ESTRAGON. I was dreaming I was happy.

VLADIMIR. That passed the time.

ESTRAGON. I was dreaming that——

VLADIMIR. Don't tell me! [*Silence.*] I wonder is he really blind.

ESTRAGON. Blind? Who?

VLADIMIR. Pozzo.

ESTRAGON. Blind?

VLADIMIR. He told us he was blind.

ESTRAGON. Well what about it?

VLADIMIR. It seemed to me he saw us.

ESTRAGON. You dreamt it. [*Pause.*] Let's go. We can't. Ah! [*Pause.*] Are you sure it wasn't him?

VLADIMIR. Who?

ESTRAGON. Godot.

VLADIMIR. But who?

ESTRAGON. Pozzo.

VLADIMIR. Not at all! Not at all! [*Pause.*] Not at all.

ESTRAGON. I suppose I might as well get up. [*He gets up painfully.*] Ow! Didi!

VLADIMIR. I don't know what to think any more.

ESTRAGON. My feet! [*He sits down, tries to take off his boots.*] Help me!

VLADIMIR. Was I sleeping, while the others suffered? Am I sleeping now? Tomorrow when I wake, or think I do, what shall I say of today? That with Estragon, my friend, at this place, until the fall of night, I waited for Godot? That Pozzo passed, with his carrier, and talked to us? Probably. But in all that what truth will there be? [ESTRAGON, *having struggled with his boots in vain, is dozing off again.* VLADIMIR *stares at him.*] He'll know nothing. He'll tell me about the blows he received and I'll give him a carrot. [*Pause.*] Astride of a grave and a difficult birth. Down in the hole, lingeringly, the grave-digger puts on the forceps. We have time to grow old. The air is full of our cries. [*He listens.*] But habit is a great deadener. [*He looks again at* ESTRAGON.] At me too someone is looking, of me too someone is saying, He is sleeping, he knows nothing, let him sleep on. [*Pause.*] I can't go on! [*Pause.*] What have I said?

> [*He goes feverishly to and fro, halts finally at extreme left, broods. Enter* BOY *right. He halts. Silence.*

BOY. Please, Mister—[VLADIMIR *turns.*] Mr. Albert?——

VLADIMIR. Off we go again. [*Pause.*] Do you not recognize me?

BOY. No, sir.

VLADIMIR. It wasn't you came yesterday.

BOY. No, sir.

VLADIMIR. This is your first time.

BOY. Yes, sir. [*Silence.*

VLADIMIR. You have a message from Mr. Godot.

BOY. Yes, sir.

VLADIMIR. He won't come this evening.

BOY. No sir.

VLADIMIR. But he'll come tomorrow.

BOY. Yes, sir.

VLADIMIR. Without fail.

BOY. Yes, sir. [*Silence.*

VLADIMIR. Did you meet anyone?

BOY. No, sir.

VLADIMIR. Two other—[*he hesitates*]—men?

BOY. I didn't see anyone, sir. [*Silence.*

VLADIMIR. What does he do, Mr. Godot? [*Silence.*] Do you hear me?

BOY. Yes, sir.

VLADIMIR. Well?

BOY. He does nothing, sir. [*Silence.*

VLADIMIR. How is your brother?

BOY. He's sick, sir.

VLADIMIR. Perhaps it was he came yesterday.

BOY. I don't know, sir. [*Silence.*

VLADIMIR [*softly*]. Has he a beard, Mr. Godot?

BOY. Yes, sir.

VLADIMIR. Fair or—[*he hesitates*]—or black?

BOY. I think it's white, sir. [*Silence.*

VLADIMIR. Christ have mercy on us! [*Silence.*

BOY. What am I to say to Mr. Godot, sir?

VLADIMIR. Tell him—[*he hesitates*]—tell him you saw me and that—[*he hesitates*]—that you saw me. [*Pause.* VLADIMIR *advances, the* BOY *recoils.* VLADIMIR *halts, the* BOY *halts.*] You're sure you saw me, eh, you won't come and tell me tomorrow that you never saw me before?

> *Silence.* VLADIMIR *makes a sudden spring forward, the* BOY *avoids him and exit running. Silence. The sun sets, the moon rises. As before.* VLADIMIR *stands motionless and bowed.* ESTRAGON *wakes, takes off his boots, gets up with them in his hands, goes and puts them down centre front, goes towards* VLADIMIR, *looks at him.*

ESTRAGON. What's wrong with you?

VLADIMIR. Nothing.

ESTRAGON. I'm going.

VLADIMIR. So am I.

ESTRAGON. Was I long asleep?

VLADIMIR. I don't know. [*Silence.*

ESTRAGON. Where shall we go?

VLADIMIR. Not far.

ESTRAGON. O yes, let's go far away from here.

VLADIMIR. We can't.

ESTRAGON. Why not?

VLADIMIR. We have to come back tomorrow.

ESTRAGON. What for?

VLADIMIR. To wait for Godot.

ESTRAGON. Ah! [*Pause.*] He didn't come?

VLADIMIR. No.

ESTRAGON. And now it's too late.

VLADIMIR. Yes, now it's night.

ESTRAGON. And if we dropped him? [*Pause.*] If we dropped him.

VLADIMIR. He'd punish us. [*Silence. He looks at the tree.*] Everything's dead but the tree.

ESTRAGON [*looking at the tree*]. What is it?

VLADIMIR. It's the tree.

ESTRAGON. Yes, but what kind?

VLADIMIR. I don't know. A willow.

[ESTRAGON *draws* VLADIMIR *towards the tree. They stand motionless before it. Silence.*

ESTRAGON. Why don't we hang ourselves?

VLADIMIR. With what?

ESTRAGON. You haven't got a bit of rope?

VLADIMIR. No.

ESTRAGON. Then we can't.

VLADIMIR. Let's go.

ESTRAGON. Wait, there's my belt.

VLADIMIR. It's too short.

ESTRAGON. You could hang on to my legs.

VLADIMIR. And who'd hang on to mine?

ESTRAGON. True.

VLADIMIR. Show all the same. [ESTRAGON *loosens the cord that holds up his trousers which, much too big for him, fall about his ankles. They look at the cord.*] That might do at a pinch. But is it strong enough?

ESTRAGON. We'll soon see. Here.

[*They each take an end of the cord and pull. It breaks. They almost fall.*

VLADIMIR. Not worth a curse.   [*Silence.*

ESTRAGON. You say we have to come back tomorrow?

VLADIMIR. Yes.

ESTRAGON. Then we can bring a good bit of rope.

VLADIMIR. Yes.   [*Silence.*

ESTRAGON. Didi.

VLADIMIR. Yes.

ESTRAGON. I can't go on like this.

VLADIMIR. That's what you think.

ESTRAGON. If we parted? That might be better for us.

VLADIMIR. We'll hang ourselves tomorrow. [*Pause.*] Unless Godot comes.

ESTRAGON. And if he comes?

VLADIMIR. We'll be saved.

> VLADIMIR *takes off his hat* (LUCKY'S) *peers inside it, feels about inside it, shakes it, knocks on the crown, puts it on again.*

ESTRAGON. Well? Shall we go?

VLADIMIR. Pull on your trousers.

ESTRAGON. What?

VLADIMIR. Pull on your trousers.

ESTRAGON. You want me to pull off my trousers?

VLADIMIR. Pull ON your trousers.

ESTRAGON [*realizing his trousers are down*]. True.

> [*He pulls up his trousers. Silence.*

VLADIMIR. Well? Shall we go?

ESTRAGON. Yes, let's go.   [*They do not move.*

POINTS FOR DISCUSSION

1. Find some examples of humour in the extract and examine their dramatic function.
2. What is the significance of the title—several times repeated in the dialogue—*Waiting for Godot*?
3. To what extent do Vladimir and Estragon talk at cross purposes?
4. Are there any parts of the dialogue that could be described as philosophic?
5. Can you see any parallel between the relations of Lucky with Pozzo and those of Vladimir and Estragon with Godot?
6. Can you suggest any reasons why Pozzo is made to be so astonishingly cruel to Lucky?
7. Why do you think Beckett makes Pozzo blind on his second appearance?
8. 'He thinks of nothing but himself.' Is there anything more in Pozzo than selfishness?
9. Is there any significance in the names that Estragon tries out on Pozzo?
10. What is the significance of the episode with the Boy?
11. Would you call this a religious or an irreligious play?
12. Is there anything in the play that can be said to make it a mirror of our times?

IN CONCLUSION

AFTER reading plays which cover a period of more than two thousand years, our final question may well concern the contribution which drama has made to the literature of nations. To interpret life has ever been the aim of drama, and to this may be attributed its enduring popularity. Through the study, and more especially through the acting, of plays, it is possible to become imaginatively identified with characters whose emotions and experiences have a perfection rarely to be found in life itself. This does not remove the experiences of drama from those of life, but rather brings the two closer together. It is the imperfections of human experiences which make it impossible for one man to understand and identify himself with the personality of another; and drama passes beyond these imperfections to emotions and situations which belong to mankind, although they may be given an intensely individual expression. It was the belief of Aristotle that, in the true performance of a tragedy, the crude emotions of the audience were absorbed into the perfect expression of these emotions in the drama, where they were cleansed and purified of their imperfections. Such a catharsis may be possible only when a great play is greatly acted, but every true drama enlarges the bounds of human experience so that actors and audience become newly aware of the significance of human personality, and of the acts by which that personality is expressed. To interpret a play is to become better able to interpret life.

PRINTED IN GREAT BRITAIN
AT THE UNIVERSITY PRESS, OXFORD
BY VIVIAN RIDLER
PRINTER TO THE UNIVERSITY